READ YOUR BIBLE ONE BOOK AT A TIME

Read Your Bible One Book at a Time

A Refreshing Way to Read God's Word
With New Insight and Meaning

WOODROW KROLL

SERVANT PUBLICATIONS
ANN ARBOR, MICHIGAN

Vine Books is an imprint of Servant Publications especially designed to serve evangelical Christians.

Servant Publications Mission Statement

We are dedicated to publishing books that spread the gospel of Jesus Christ, help Christians to live in accordance with that gospel, promote renewal in the church, and bear witness to Christian unity.

All Scripture quotations are taken from The New King James Version®, Copyright 1982 by Thomas Nelson, Inc. Used by permission.

Published by Servant Publications
P.O. Box 8617
Ann Arbor, Michigan 48107
www.servantpub.com

Cover design: Alan Furst, Inc. Minneapolis, Minn.

02 03 04 05 06 10 9 8 7 6 5 4 3 2 1

Printed in the United States of America
ISBN 1-56955-328-9

Library of Congress Cataloging-in-Publication Data

Kroll, Woodrow Michael, 1944-
Read your Bible one book at a time : a refreshing way to read God's word with new insight and meaning / Woodrow Kroll.
    p. cm.
ISBN 1-56955-328-9
 1. Bible--Reading. I. Title.
BS617 .K76 2002
220'.071--dc21

2002003198

Dedicated to

friends and supporters
of Back to the Bible
around the world,
people who have prayed
consistently and given of their
resources faithfully so we could
teach the Word
and touch the world.

Contents

Acknowledgments

There's good reason why people refer to the ministry of Back to the Bible as "the Bible teacher to the world." With offices in a dozen countries, broadcasts in twenty-five languages (seven of the ten most frequently spoken languages), and forty-nine skilled and dedicated national Bible teachers around the world, Back to the Bible is leading people into a dynamic relationship with God in every corner of the globe. And we do it with just one book—the Bible.

Our passion is to see people read God's Word and be changed by it. Whether by radio, video, literature, television, the Internet, or in person, we teach God's Word so you know what the Bible says, what it means, and how it applies to your life. We believe it is incredibly important to get people into their Bibles, for "faith comes by hearing, and hearing by the word of God" (Rom. 10:17). This book is another salvo in our battle against Bible illiteracy.

I want to thank all the Back to the Bible staff who assisted me in preparing this book. My wife, Linda, gave me the assistance of her encouragement. Cathy Strate provided administrative assistance, Allen Bean provided research assistance, and Rachel Derowitsch gave editorial assistance. Many of our staff timed themselves while reading a book of the Bible so we would have an accurate average of the time required to read each book. Others assisted in numerous ways. Everything we do at Back to the Bible is truly a team effort. Thanks to you all.

Reading your Bible one book at a time is not just a frivolous suggestion. I've done it myself and found it to be amazingly helpful. And, believe me, it's not as intimidating as you may think. In this book you'll find tools and plenty of encouragement to help you discover the unique benefits of reading a book of the Bible as you would a letter, all the way through in one sitting. Now it's up to you. Just do it.

Woodrow Kroll
Lincoln, Nebraska

Introduction

Have you ever come home in the evening after a long day, clicked on the TV, and found yourself in the middle of a movie? You've missed the first half hour, so you missed the setup. What's the plot? Who are these characters? How do they relate to one another?

Or maybe you're quietly watching your favorite TV program when the phone rings. It's your friend from work and she wants to talk. You mute the television. Yak, yak, yak. Finally you give up and just turn it off. You talk for almost an hour. You like your friend, but you're a little upset because you're never going to find out how your program ended.

Some people read their Bible this way. They pick it up, begin in the middle of a book, and wonder why they can't figure out the story line. Or they let everything in life interrupt them. They read a chapter or two, lay God's Word aside, and never get back to it to find out how the story ends.

Help Is Here

You've probably struggled to make sense of the Bible, as everyone has. Maybe this book will help you in that endeavor. Reading whole books of the Bible in one sitting sounds like a crazy idea, but it works. Toward the end of the nineteenth century, when Bishop Wright was preaching with conviction that God didn't intend men to fly, he never suspected that his two sons, Wilbur and Orville, were out in the barn hatching a crazy flying contraption. Sometimes the more unusual the idea, the more likely it is to work.

Read Your Bible One Book at a Time is a refreshing way to discover he story line, uncover the plot, and find out how it all turns out. How does the plan work? It's embarrassingly simple. Just read one book of your Bible all the way through in one sitting. "You mean ...?" Yes, read the whole book. Get the full story the writer intended you to get. Start at the beginning and don't quit until you reach the end. It sounds a little nutty, I know, but don't dismiss it until you've tried it. It's not really a novel idea, except as it applies to reading the Bible.

"Can't do it. Don't have time!" you protest. I hear you, but consider this. How long is your favorite sitcom? Probably thirty minutes, right? And what about programs like *Dateline, Law & Order,* and *Touched by an Angel*? They're sixty minutes each. Last Christmas I kicked off my shoes, eased back into my lounge chair, and watched three classics that air every Christmas season: *It's a Wonderful Life* (131 minutes), *Miracle on 34th Street* (94 minutes), and *A Christmas Story* (94 minutes). I watched them from beginning to end, from black screen to black again. The whole movie. In one sitting. Are you getting the picture? I watched these movies from start to finish, not just a few minutes at a time with the notion of coming back the next day to watch a little more. I followed the story line, got to know the characters and their lives, and even got the point at the end of the movie (well, maybe not with *A Christmas Story*).

Prepare to Be Amazed

Let's apply that principle to reading the Bible. If you wanted to read one book of the Bible—the whole book, beginning to end—which ones could you read during the same time it takes to watch *It's a Wonderful Life?* Hold on to your hat. You could read any book of the Bible except twelve. Only a dozen books of the Bible take longer to read than watching that classic Christmas movie.

Nearly forty books of the Bible can be read in an hour or less.

Half the books of the Bible can be read in less than thirty minutes.

And twenty-six books can be read in fifteen minutes or less.

That's pretty amazing for a book that many people think is too massive to read. When you think about it, time really isn't the problem when it comes to reading the Bible. It's a good excuse, but not good enough. How much we read of the only book God ever wrote depends mostly on how much of it we want to read. Reading God's Word is less dependent on our schedule and more dependent on our desire and discipline.

Let's be honest. Some books of the Bible can be pretty difficult. John Bunyan, author of the classic Christian allegory *Pilgrim's Progress,* said, "I have sometimes seen more in a line of the Bible than I could well tell how to stand under, and yet at another time the whole Bible hath been to me as dry as a stick." Have you felt the same way? Likely you have. If someone like John Bunyan had difficulty reading portions of the Scripture, why not people like you and me?

I don't know anyone who can breeze through the first dozen chapters of 1 Chronicles or any of the Book of Ezekiel. Breeze through? Not on your life. Benefit from? Absolutely.

The great prayer of Jabez (found in 1 Chronicles 4:9-10), one of the most inspiring passages in the Old Testament, occurs right in the middle of an almost endless list of names recorded in that book. Fail to read 1 Chronicles and you miss Jabez's wonderful prayer. Besides, the rest of the book is the readable and enjoyable story of Israel's most famous king, David. So, even 1 Chronicles is worth the read. And buried deep within the somewhat obscure prophecies of Ezekiel is the call for a man to stand in the gap for God (22:30), the story of Lucifer's pride and fall from God's presence (28:12-17), and that fascinating image of the valley of dry bones coming to life again (37). It's really great stuff!

Eleven books of the Old Testament can be read in fifteen minutes or less.

Some portions of the Bible may be tougher to read than others, but you can do it. And while it may not be evident at first, you will benefit from reading every book of the Bible. Only those who have not read have not benefited. So, pick a place (a place you won't be disturbed); choose a reading plan (check out the plans in the appendices at the back of this book), or decide which book you want to read; make sure you have allowed sufficient time in your schedule to read the book all the way through; and begin. You can do it! You can read your Bible—one book at a time.

Chapter 1

Features of This Book

I had nearly two hours to sit at the airport, so I decided to read through as much of Romans as I could. Thanks to the delay, I read the whole thing, amazed at how much everything fit together. I'm so used to reading bits and pieces that I'd lost sight of the "big ideas" included. It was so exciting to rediscover a familiar portion of God's Word.

—Barbara Gerhart

This book contains a one-page synopsis of each book of the Bible. The synopses give you information about the author, the audience, the subject, and the scope of the sixty-six books that comprise God's Word. They will help you understand what the author wants you to know and do. For instance, the "three keys" section highlights the most important people, chapters, and verses in the book. Look for these as you read, and you'll be able to see around the next bend and know who or what awaits you there. And the book profile is like a stat sheet, giving you the vital statistics of each book and approximately how long it will take to read it.

The "what to look for" section points out some of the features that are unique to that book. In every Bible book you'll find Jesus Christ described, if you look with the eyes of faith. He is the thread that is woven through every book, holding each one to the Bible's theme of

God's redemption. That's why, after His resurrection, with two friends on the road to the village of Emmaus, Jesus began with the writings of Moses and all the prophets and "expounded to them in all the Scriptures the things concerning Himself" (Luke 24:27).

In every book you'll discover interesting, entertaining, and important people and their stories. You'll also uncover tidbits and truths that will make you want to read the book again. Read all the books first, and then go back and read some of your favorites again.

Dating the Book

Some of the features highlighted in each book are certain. For example, the number of chapters is factual; the scope of the book is established. These things will not change and are beyond question. But others are more difficult to pinpoint with the same degree of certainty. Dating when a book was written, for instance, can be a bit tricky and deserves a little more explanation.

Since the exact date of composition is extremely difficult to determine, all dates listed are approximate. Sometimes the dates given are the dates for the author's life or ministry since we don't know during which period of his life he wrote the book. Sometimes the average of various assertions by multiple scholars is suggested.

Of all the books in the Bible, only Haggai contains only two chapters.

Often other factors were used to determine the date. We know that Lamentations, for example, had to have been written after the fall of Jerusalem in 586 B.C. but before Jeremiah was taken into captivity in

Egypt after Gedaliah's assassination (583–582 B.C.; see Jer. 43:1-7). Thus a date of 586–583 B.C. is given.

Jonah's prophecy is dated by the reign of the king during which he prophesied. We know it was during the reign of Jeroboam II (793–753 B.C.), but we cannot pinpoint it any more accurately than that.

Sometimes a date is based as much on what is not said as what is said. Nahum likely wrote between 663 and 645 B.C. The fall of Thebes (or No Amon), which occurred in 663 B.C., is mentioned in Nahum 3:8. But

Approximately 25 percent of the New Testament was authored by Paul.

nine years later, 654 B.C., Thebes was restored. Nahum's rhetorical question in 3:8 would have little force if it had been written after 654.

And, yes, sometimes we can even date the writing of a book with exact precision. For example, Haggai was written in 520 B.C. because he mentions that he wrote during the second year of King Darius, and we can date Darius exactly from historical records. For the most part, however, the dates listed for each Bible book are approximate.

Overview

One feature to aid you in understanding each book is the overview section. This gives the subject, scope, and setting of each book, with a few exceptions.

The subject identifies what the book is about, what you should expect to uncover as you read the book. For example, the subject of the Book of Ruth is that God sovereignly brings together two people who are key characters in the lineage of Jesus the Messiah. When you anticipate what you will find, each verse leads you to your discovery.

The scope identifies how much time elapsed during the events of the book. Some books of the Bible cover little time; others a great deal. In the example of Ruth, the events of this book occur during a time period of approximately twelve years. You will notice that the scope feature is not included in some books. While the four Gospels and the Book of Acts are historical in nature, and thus include the scope feature, all of the epistles are letters and thus are

Approximately 25 percent of the Old Testament was authored by Moses.

epistolary, not historical, in nature. They were written at one sitting and are largely doctrinal in content, and thus the scope feature is omitted. The Book of Revelation is prophetic in nature and thus is future history. As such, judging the scope is easy for the seven years of tribulation and one thousand years of the Millennium, but since this book also includes eternity, specifying the scope is impossible.

The setting describes the geographical or national backdrop of the book. It explains where the events of the book take place. The setting of Ruth is first in Moab, the land east of the Dead Sea, and then Bethlehem in Judea west of the Dead Sea.

Each of these features enhances both our anticipation and our understanding of the book we are reading, and by reading in one sitting, we gain an appreciation of the subject, scope, and setting of the book.

Reading Plans

At the end of this book, in the appendices, are several reading plans to help you read your Bible one book at a time. The five-star plans, like five-star hotels, are best. These plans will enable you to read a book of the Bible in one sitting. Appendix D is the one-year Sunday reading plan. This plan guides you in reading a different book, or books if they are smaller, each Sunday. If you are looking for an alternative to Sunday TV, this is it. If you are football-deprived during the off-season and want get to know God better, this is the plan for you. Of course, you could do the reading on Saturday, or any other day of the week, but this plan will help you read at least one book of the Bible each week in one sitting.

Appendix E is a six-month reading plan that helps you plan to read an entire book of the Bible on just two days during the week and on Sunday. Again, these could be any days that fit your schedule. This plan is also a five-star schedule because in a six-month period you read the whole Bible one book at a time. You get the same benefit as the one-year plan, but you get it in half the time.

Appendix F is a very aggressive reading plan for those of you looking for a challenge and who are interested in getting a complete overview of the Bible in a short time. This plan calls for you to read Monday, Wednesday, and Friday one week, Tuesday and Thursday the next week, plus both Saturday and Sunday on the weekends. Using this schedule allows you to complete the Bible in three months. It, too, is a five-star plan because it guides you into reading each book in one sitting, which is always best for understanding the story line or the logic of a book.

Don't have time to read one of those big books in one sitting? No problem. Appendix G presents a plan that schedules your reading in half-hour blocks. This is a wonderful way to read your Bible if you are not able to sit for longer periods. Even though you read only a half hour at a time, you read the book on adjacent days, and that will reduce the potential of forgetting what you read the day before. It's not as good as reading one book at a time, but it's close and it will give you much greater continuity than if you read the book in an occasional manner.

Choose a plan that best fits your lifestyle, or devise your own plan. Each plan tells you the average time needed to read a book and a place for you to record the date when you have completed it. The important thing is that you read through the books of your Bible in a way that gives you fresh insight that you would be denied by simply reading a chapter or two here and there. If the plan is yours, the benefit will be yours as well.

See What's in There

Reading your Bible one book at a time is not the fast track to deep insight. This isn't the way to do Bible study. You aren't taking notes, memorizing, or even meditating on what you've read. You are simply reading an entire book to get an overview of it. But don't make this a speed-reading contest. It is more of a marathon than a sprint.

When you sit down with a commentary on one side and your computer on the other, and you read your Bible to deepen your own spiritual maturity, that's one thing. When you read your Bible just to find out "what's in there," that's another. Reading your Bible one book at a time, in one sitting, is of the "what's in there" variety. Most people do not know much about the Bible because they rarely read it. This unique approach will help you remedy that problem, and have some fun in the process.

Chapter 2

Seven Sensible Reasons for Reading One Book at a Time

I recently read the Book of 1 John in one sitting. It was helpful to see some themes repeatedly appearing throughout the entire book. The one that struck me most was how we can know for sure we are "in Him"—by our belief about Jesus, by loving our brothers, and by living righteously.

—*Chad Williams*

Reading through an entire book of the Bible in one sitting sounds like a daunting task. Even some of the smaller books can challenge our concentration skills. Mention to your friends that you are reading all the way through the Bible one book at a time and their blank stares will be unmistakable. They'll think you're not the brightest bulb in the pack. So why should you read a book of the Bible all the way through at one time? Let's think of some sensible reasons.

1. Continuity
Reading your Bible one book at a time provides continuity in what you read. Continuity means uninterrupted connection, succession, or union. It's when you pass from one element to another, almost without notice. The Bible is like that. When you read an entire book at one sitting, you discover continuity in God's Word you may never have realized existed.

If you read only the first couple of chapters in Acts, for instance, you might think the book is all about the Jerusalem church. You'd be convinced the major players were Peter, John, Stephen, and others in Jerusalem. You would never guess places like Philippi, Ephesus, Athens, and Antioch would play such significant roles in the spread of Christianity. That's because reading only a few chapters robs you of continuity. If you never read past chapter eight, you would never know the influence the apostle Paul had on the developing church. That's continuity. When you read the whole book at one time, you not only find out where the church began but also where it was moving. That's continuity. The flow of history in the New

Fifteen books of the Old Testament contain ten or fewer chapters, and only four contain more than fifty chapters.

Testament church moves from Jerusalem to Antioch, and from there to Macedonia and to the rest of the world. The flow of history moves from Peter and Stephen to Barnabas and Paul; eventually, Paul predominates (contrast Acts 11:30; 12:25; 13:1-2; 14:14; and 15:12, 25 with Acts 13:43, 46, 50 and 15:2, 22, 36). Reading all the way through Acts helps you navigate this flow of history and appreciate continuity.

2. The Thread of Truth
The writers of the Bible were no less skillful than good writers of the twenty-first century. They knew how to thread truth through their writing and not let it bunch up at the beginning or at the end. If you read a chapter or two at a time, you miss unraveling this "thread of truth." If you read the whole book at a time, it becomes amazingly evident to you.

> *Once you have read the Gospels and Acts, you are almost 60 percent finished reading the New Testament.*

Predominant in Paul's epistle to the Ephesian Christians, for example, is the association of the believer with Christ, the Head of the Church. The tiny but pregnant phrase "in Christ" is threaded throughout Ephesians to illustrate that association (1:1, 3, 10; 2:6, 10, 13; 3:6). Read only a chapter or two and that thread is lost on you. Read the whole book and it's tied to you forever.

Similarly, the Book of Hebrews is threaded with contrasts between Christ and others in order to demonstrate the superiority of Christ. Jesus is superior to angels (1:4-8); the heavens and earth (1:10-12); mankind (2:6-8); Moses (3:1-6); the priesthood of Aaron (5:1-6); the Levitical priesthood (7:11-22); the old covenant (8:6-13); the high priest (9:6-12); the Old Testament sacrifices (9:13-15); and those Christian martyrs who preceded us (12:1). This "thread of truth" will escape you entirely if you do not read this book through in one sitting.

If you don't read the whole book at one time, you see only segments of the thread and not the whole. Read your Bible one book at a time and tie a knot at the end of the thread when you finish.

3. The Full Story

In Charles Dickens' classic *A Christmas Carol*, does Scrooge remain a miser all his life? No, of course not, but how do you know? You know because you have read the whole story—and probably not in multiple installments. You read it in one sitting.

The books of the Bible are like *A Christmas Carol*. The Gospels of Matthew and Luke record the events surrounding the birth of the babe in a Bethlehem stable and the crucifixion and burial of that same babe, now the Christ of Calvary. To get the full story of Jesus' life you must read the Gospels all the way through. And like *A Christmas Carol,* the best way to get the whole story is to read it from start to finish.

If you don't read *A Christmas Carol* in one sitting, you'll miss the joy of transformation (the miserly Scrooge). If you don't read an entire Gospel in one sitting, you'll miss the joy of resurrection (Jesus Christ, the risen Lord). But read one book of your Bible all the way through at one time and you'll get the full story.

4. Confusing Events

Let's face it. There are lots of mysteries in the Bible—lots of things we find difficult to understand. Sometimes events seem confusing, even contradictory. Reading a Bible book in one sitting reduces the confusion and helps you take quantum leaps in biblical understanding. Think of this example.

You are probably familiar with the story of Jesus feeding the five thousand. But are you equally familiar with the story of the feeding of the four thousand? Maybe not. So was it five thousand or four thousand? Are these the same event? Do they just reflect a sloppy job by the author in recording the numbers? Or are these two separate events?

Read a book at one time—Matthew, for instance—and the answer becomes clear. These are two separate events. The facts of the two accounts are quite different. In the feeding of the 5,000 there were five loaves and two fish. The number of baskets of food that remained was twelve, and Jesus immediately departed to the mountain to pray afterward (Matt. 14:16-23; Mark 6:38-46; Luke 9:13-18; John 6:5-15). In the feeding of the 4,000 there were seven loaves and a few fish. The number of baskets that remained was seven, and Jesus immediately departed by boat to Magdala (Matt. 15:30-39; Mark 8:1-9). In fact, if you read far enough in the Gospels, Jesus actually contrasts these two events, proving they were separate incidents (Matt. 16:9-10; Mark 8:19-20).

Don't be confused about biblical events. Read the whole book and you'll get the whole story. You'll be able to come to accurate and certain conclusions about events that confuse others.

5. Elapsed Time

When you are reading your Bible, do you ever get the sense that you have no idea how much time has elapsed between the events of the first chapter and the last chapter of a book? That's true for most of us.

Seventeen books in the New Testament contain less than ten chapters, and only two contain more than twenty-five chapters.

Are we talking about days or years of elapsed time? You cannot tell by looking at the number of chapters in a book. Isaiah has sixty-six chapters, but the elapsed time for the events he records is only about sixty-five years, essentially one year per chapter. In contrast, Genesis has only fifty chapters but covers thousands of years.

Get ready for an eye-opener. The Book of Judges has just twenty-two chapters, but the elapsed time of the events recorded there is approximately 550 years, more than half a millennium. The reason is that there are huge blocks of time between most of the judges, during which Israel lived at peace with her enemies. For example, after God raised up Othniel, the first judge, Israel experienced forty years of peace (Judg. 3:11). Then, for eighteen years God's people were under the oppression of Moab's king Eglon (v. 14). As a result, God commissioned the next judge, Ehud (v. 15). And while we don't know how long Ehud's political and military leadership lasted, we do know that after it finished, Israel experienced eighty years of peace with the nations around her. Forty years of peace. Eighteen years of oppression. The years of Ehud's ministry. Eighty years of peace. You can see how quickly the time adds up.

You have to read the entire Book of Judges to sense the progress of history over five and a half centuries. If you don't, it's just one story after another, with little or no sense of the time that it takes for those stories to play out.

6. Follow the Logic

Some books of the Bible are difficult to follow. There doesn't seem to be any historical sequence or logic to them. Take the Book of Revelation, for example. If you try to follow the Apocalypse chronologically, you'll be as skittish as a chameleon scampering across a plaid tablecloth. It isn't written in historical sequence. Chapters later in the book actually relate to events earlier in the book. It's hard to follow the history and certainly difficult to follow the logic.

But not all books are like that. Paul's logic in Romans is impeccable. He uses the tactics of a trial lawyer to present his case for salvation. He begins with condemnation. All humanity is in desperate need of salvation (1:1–3:20), and Paul concludes that all the world is lost and guilty before God (3:19). That

One book in the Old Testament and four books in the New Testament contain only one chapter.

established, the apostle moves on to the subject of salvation. God justifies us and declares us righteous in response to our faith (3:21–8:39). Next, the issue is vindication. Paul answers the question, "If God made a covenant with Israel, how can Israel be condemned with the rest of the world?" (9:1–11:36). Having answered the objections of his countrymen, Paul concludes his argument with an exhortation, a treatment of how we should live in light of God's gracious salvation (12:1–16:27).

Paul's logic is easily followed, but unless you read the entire epistle at one time, you lose this impeccable logic and may fail to reach the proper conclusion. Reading your Bible one book at a time makes the difference.

7. Like Reading a Letter

Do you remember receiving letters from friends back home when you were away? When you received your letter from a friend or sweetheart, what did you do with it? You read it, of course. Maybe you even reread it, perhaps a dozen times. But did you read it all? Did you read it all at once, from start to finish? Of course you did. You didn't just read a couple of pages and say, "Well, that's enough for now. I'll read more tomorrow." Letters are meant to be read through and enjoyed. They are not meant to be partially read in daily installments.

While much of the Old Testament is historical, much of the New Testament is epistolary—written as letters from a Christian friend. The four Gospels, Acts, and the Book of Revelation weren't written as letters (although Luke addresses his account of Jesus' life and work to his friend Theophilus, and Revelation contains letters to seven churches). The other books of the New Testament clearly are epistles. That's twenty-one books out of twenty-seven written as letters. If you do not read letters from your friends a page or two at a time, why would you read Paul's or Peter's or John's letters a page at a time? That's not the way it's supposed to be done.

Reading your Bible one book at a time holds unique benefits for you. Unfortunately, we have become accustomed to reading in installments.

Our Bible-reading time is usually a chapter or two, a daily inspirational reading, some time in prayer, and then it's off to the races. We rarely get all we could from the writers of Scripture because we don't read all they said. You can change that. There's a better way. Read your Bible one book at a time.

Chapter 3

Hints on How to Succeed

Before our pastor began a series on Ephesians, we devoted an entire worship service to reading that wonderful epistle. Six readers took turns. At natural break points, we sang related hymns and choruses. This helped us begin to grasp the big picture of Paul's letter to the Ephesians. My young children were surprised at how fast the service went.

—Steve Nickel

Reading a book of the Bible all the way through not only enhances your understanding of the book, but it also gives you a "feel" for what the author wants you to know. It's the way he wrote it and how he wants you to read it. But as in any guide to reading through the Bible, the seeds of failure are sown among the seeds of success. How will you eliminate the bad seed while you're cultivating the good seed? Here are some suggestions.

Think Outside the Box

Who ever heard of reading a book of the Bible all the way through in one sitting? It sounds like such an impossible task. But it isn't. This is not the usual way people approach reading through the Bible.

Generally, we make plans to read through the Bible in a year. You've probably tried it and so have I. Sometimes we are successful. Often we begin expectantly on January 1 and read faithfully until, say, the middle of February. And then? Well, you know. Let's face it. Reading the Bible through in a year is not as easy as mindlessly watching your favorite sitcom, but it's a whole lot more beneficial.

Reading through your Bible one book at a time does not require a year. In fact, there is no minimum or maximum time to do this. But it does require you to think outside of the box. Most people believe the books of the Bible are too long, the language too difficult to understand, and those names—some of them are simply unpronounceable. But as we have seen, most books are not as long as people think. And the language used in the Bible can be quite user-friendly, especially if you read from your favorite translation or a new translation in which the language is more contemporary. And as for the names of people and places? Well, give it your best shot. If you stumble over them you have joined the majority of people who also have stumbled over

Fifteen books of the New Testament can be read in fifteen minutes or less.

them. We do the same today when we travel to Russia or China or some part of the world where the names are not familiar to us.

Don't just be envious of those who read their Bible with great benefit. Join them. When you read your Bible one book at a time, you're defying generations of traditional schedules for reading your Bible. Think inside the Book, but outside the box.

Take the Average Reading Time Seriously

The average reading time is, of course, an average; it's a general guide. You may find that you read each book of the Bible in much less time than is listed. Or you may need more time. It doesn't matter. This is not a speed-reading contest. People read at different rates and that's okay. The average reading times are listed only to help you know approximately how much time to set aside in your day in order to read all the way through the book. Do pay attention to these times. You'll only be frustrated if you try to read a book when you know you don't have time to get through it. Choose another book, a shorter book, to read in the time you have.

Be honest. You probably can't read Isaiah between the time you finish dinner and snuggle in to watch *Who Wants to Be a Millionaire?* You'll need to find a larger block of time to read a major book like this. Plan ahead. Take the required reading time seriously. It is provided with each book for your benefit.

Mix Up Your Reading

The books of the Bible vary greatly, both in length and readability. Try to mix up your reading so you are not "plowing through" a series of books that may not be easy to read. I don't recommend reading Jeremiah, Lamentations, and Ezekiel on the same weekend. That may be a little much. But you could read Jeremiah and Lamentations the same weekend, at two different times perhaps, if you carved out some free time. These two books, Jeremiah and Lamentations, written by the same man and relating to the same events, naturally go together.

Use wisdom in selecting which books you will read and how closely together you will read them. Remember, this is an adventure, not an endurance race. Some books are going to be more exciting than others. Mix them up and benefit from all of them.

Check out the reading plans in the appendices of this book. They mix the reading so that you never read two of the "big" books back-to-back. The books are not listed in chronological order, alphabetical order, or even canonical order (the order in which they occur in the Bible). The order doesn't matter when you read your Bible one book at a time. What matters is that you gain fresh insight into a particular book by reading it all the way through in one sitting.

Control Your Environment

You are in control. You choose when you will read, what you will read, where you will read, and how long you will read. Control your environment as completely as possible, and that puts you in charge.

I first began reading each book of the Bible in one sitting while flying on airplanes. I hung a stopwatch around my neck, buckled in, waited for "wheels up," and then began to read. On shorter, domestic flights I'd read shorter books. On transatlantic flights I'd read longer books. Once a flight attendant saw my stopwatch and asked, "Are you timing our service?" I smiled and joked, "No, if I were doing that, I'd need a calendar." We both laughed and then I confessed, "Actually I'm timing how long it takes me to read the Book of Job." Apparently satisfied with my answer, she went about her duties. But an airplane isn't the best place to read with understanding. I really wasn't fully in control of my environment. Meals were served, people jostled by me, the captain warned of turbulence, the lights dimmed so others could see the in-flight movie. I had to find another place and get better control of my environment.

For optimal success, find a place to read where you won't be disturbed. You need a quiet place, perhaps an out-of-the-way place. You also need a quiet time to read. You can't do this while tending to the children, but you could do it while they are taking a nap. Find a quiet place and a quiet time. Switch off the telephone. Keep the disturbances at bay. Concentrate on what you read and, for best results, read all the way to the end of the book before you stop. You're going to be surprised how much you learn.

Do Some Debriefing

When Bob Mitchell, a coworker at Back to the Bible, read all the way through some books of the Bible, he noted, "It takes a fair degree of self-discipline to just keep reading when you'd rather underline, jot notes, look up some cross-references, etc. But it does whet your appetite to do these things in the near future."

He's right. It will require self-discipline to not interrupt yourself. But after you have finished reading a Bible book, don't rush away from it. That's the time to make your "big picture" notes. You were not meditating on what the author said while you were reading, but as soon as you finish and have a good handle on the message of the book as a whole, that's the time to make some notes, write your impressions, and craft a couple of paragraphs about what that book says, what it means, and how it applies to your life today. That's the time to meditate.

Let the whole of what you've read sink in. Let it marinate in your mind. Reading your Bible one book at a time doesn't mean you read without thinking; it just means you do your thinking after you have read everything the author has to say to you.

Of course, it takes discipline to read an entire book, but every good thing does. Try reading through the books of your Bible one at a time. Come to appreciate this refreshing way to read God's Word with new insight and meaning. You will get an exhilarating sense of accomplishment once you do, but don't read these books just to mark them off the list on your Bible-reading schedule. Read your Bible one book at a time to absorb what can be absorbed only when you see the whole forest and not just a few trees. The benefit is worth the effort.

Chapter 4

It's Time to Get Started

I read through a book of the Bible in one sitting with my eight-year-old son. I read and he listened and asked questions. A couple hours later we finished. He had asked tons of great questions and said, "Dad, that was fun. The time went so fast."

—*Martin Jones*

Enough talk. It's time to get started. Each page that follows is dedicated to one book of the Bible. Give each page a once-over before you begin and keep it handy as you read, especially to remind you of the key verses and chapters and what to look for in your reading.

Can you do it? Can you read each book of the Bible, one book at a time? Of course you can. Ezekiel, Jeremiah, the Psalms, and a few others will be a challenge, but ask the Lord to make them meaningful to you and be on the lookout for what God has to say to you. After all, He wrote only one book. Don't you think He intended you to read it?

And when you finish—after you have read all sixty-six books, one at a time—why not take a few minutes to write or e-mail us at Back to the Bible to say what exciting things God taught you by reading your Bible in this novel way? We'd be delighted to hear from you. Our weekday phone number is (402) 464-7200. You can fax us at (402) 464-7474. Or you can e-mail your response to bb@backtothebible.org. It would be great to hear from you.

And then try your hand at Back to the Bible's popular online Bible quiz. It's called The Bible Challenge and it enables you to test your Bible knowledge (at different levels) in the privacy and convenience of your home or office. Just go to www.biblechallenge.com and take the challenge!

Back to the Bible is dedicated to teaching the Word and touching the world. We are constantly seeking new ways to aid you in your personal Bible reading and study, and to challenge you to greater depths in your biblical understanding. We pray this resource is especially helpful to you.

Genesis
The Book of Beginnings

Written:
Author: Moses
Audience: the people of Israel
Date: 1450–1410 B.C.

Overview:
Subject: God's plan to restore a ruined earth as revealed through the lives of seven men—Adam, Abel, Noah, Abraham, Isaac, Jacob, and Joseph
Scope: the events of Genesis cover the period from the creation of the world to the death of Joseph
Setting: the Middle East

Three keys:
Key chapters: 1 (Creation); 6–9 (the great Flood); 12 (the call of Abraham)
Key verses: 1:1, 27; 6:8; 12:1-3; 14:18-20; 15:6; 50:20
Key people: Adam, Eve, Abel, Noah, Abraham, Melchizedek, Isaac, Jacob, Joseph, Pharaoh

Book profile:
Number of chapters: 50
Number of verses: 1,533
Average reading time: 3 hours, 10 minutes

What to look for:
- Jesus Christ as the Seed of Abraham (22:18)
- lots of "firsts," such as the first promise, first miracle, first murder, first polygamist, and first blessing
- the care and provision from God for a family through the progression of four generations

Why you should read Genesis:
When you need answers to counter the arguments of evolutionists, this book will give you God's truth on how our world began. When you are facing a decision of whether or not to follow God, let Abraham guide you. At the age of seventy-five, he made his decision and never turned back.

Exodus
The Book of Deliverance

Written:
Author: Moses
Audience: the people of Israel
Date: 1450–1410 B.C.

Overview:
Subject: the bondage and deliverance of Israel from Egypt and the giving of God's law
Scope: the events of Exodus cover about 145 years, from the birth of Moses to the setting up of the tabernacle
Setting: Egypt

Three keys:
Key chapters: 3 (the call of Moses); 12 (the Passover); 20 (the Ten Commandments)
Key verses: 3:7, 10, 13-14; 12:12-13; 20:3-17; 32:26; 33:11
Key people: Moses, Aaron, Pharaoh, Jethro, Joshua

Book profile:
Number of chapters: 40
Number of verses: 1,213
Average reading time: 2 hours, 20 minutes

What to look for:
- Jesus Christ as the Passover Lamb (12:3-8, 12-13)
- the roots of the Jewish religion in the Passover, the original code of conduct in the Ten Commandments, and detailed instructions on how to fabricate the most marvelous moveable tent in history
- God's repeated acts of redemption of His people, even when His people repeatedly complained against Him

Why you should read Exodus:
Sin is like the Pharaoh of Egypt; it holds us hostage as the Pharaoh did Israel. But when God intends to deliver us from the bondage of personal sin, we can be certain He will stop at nothing. Be encouraged. God can free you from the bondage of sin if you follow His leading.

Leviticus
The Book of Atonement

Written:
Author: Moses
Audience: the people of Israel
Date: 1450–1410 B.C.

Overview:
Subject: the bondage and deliverance of Israel from Egypt and the giving of God's Law
Scope: uncertain
Setting: Mount Sinai

Three keys:
Key chapters: 16 (the Day of Atonement); 17 (the importance of sacrificial blood)
Key verses: 11:44-45; 17:11; 18:22-23; 19:2; 20:26; 26:12
Key people: Moses, Aaron, Nadab, Abihu, Eleazar, Ithamar

Book profile:
Number of chapters: 27
Number of verses: 859
Average reading time: 2 hours, 1 minute

What to look for:
- Jesus Christ as the Great High Priest (21:10-12)
- clues to holiness—not just separation from pagan peoples and practices but a true desire to be like God
- a link between the themes of Leviticus and its New Testament counterpart, the Letter to the Hebrews

Why you should read Leviticus:
Holiness is possible. Holiness should be as important to us as it is to God. Leviticus mentions holiness more times (152) than any other book of the Bible. By reading Leviticus, you will discover God's standards for living a holy life.

Numbers
The Book of Israel's Journey

Written:
Author: Moses
Audience: the people of Israel
Date: 1406 B.C.

Overview:
Subject: Israel prepares for her decades-long wilderness journey
Scope: the events of Numbers span about forty years
Setting: Mount Sinai

Three keys:
Key chapters: 6 (Aaronic benediction); 14 (failure to believe God)
Key verses: 6:24-26; 9:8; 11:17; 13:30-31; 14:22-23; 24:17
Key people: Moses, Aaron, Miriam, Joshua, Caleb, Korah, Balaam

Book profile:
Number of chapters: 36
Number of verses: 1,288
Average reading time: 2 hours, 51 minutes

What to look for:
- Jesus Christ as the Star of Jacob (24:17)
- spiritual lessons you can learn from forty years of failure in the wilderness, failures like the spineless spies and the rebellion of Korah
- evidence that failure to believe the promises of God always results in His judgment

Why you should read Numbers:
There is a short route to victory. All of us will pass through wilderness experiences, but when we do, it is not necessary to live in them. Israel's eleven-day journey turned into a forty-year disaster because the people failed to fully trust the promises of God. Use Numbers to show a friend trapped in addiction to drugs, sex, or alcohol that obedience to God is the surest route to victory.

Deuteronomy
The Book of the Law

Written:
Author: Moses
Audience: the people of Israel
Date: 1406 B.C.

Overview:
Subject: a review of Israel's journey and guidelines for entering the Promised Land
Scope: the events of Deuteronomy cover about forty years
Setting: the east side of the Jordan River, in what is today the country of Jordan

Three keys:
Key chapters: 5 (the Ten Commandments); 29 (the Palestinian Covenant)
Key verses: 6:4; 7:9; 10:12-13; 18:18; 19:14; 29:10-13; 30:19; 33:27
Key people: Moses and Joshua

Book profile:
Number of chapters: 34
Number of verses: 959
Average reading time: 2 hours, 18 minutes

What to look for:
- Jesus Christ as the "prophet like Moses" (34:10-12)
- Deuteronomy may well have been Jesus' favorite book; look for clues that will tell you why
- not a simple restatement of the events of the Exodus and wilderness journey, but a new perspective on those events for a new generation, which was not alive when Moses received the Law on Mount Sinai

Why you should read Deuteronomy:
God's track record is a reason to trust Him. By reviewing His promises and His record of performance in Israel's history, you gain confidence that He who has kept His promises in the past will do so in the future. You can trust God.

Joshua

The Book of Canaan's Conquest

Written:
Author: Joshua
Audience: the people of Israel
Date: 1400–1350 B.C.

Overview:
Subject: Israel enters the Promised Land, claims it for God, and assigns by tribe the land as an inheritance
Scope: the events of Joshua cover about twenty-five years, from the death of Moses to the death of Joshua
Setting: the Promised Land, also called Canaan, a prime piece of real estate that covers approximately the same geographical territory as the modern state of Israel

Three keys:
Key chapters: 1 (commission of Joshua as Israel's new leader); 6 (the fall of Jericho); 24 (Joshua's farewell address)
Key verses: 1:8; 2:18; 5:13-15; 6:20, 26; 14:12; 22:5; 24:15
Key people: Joshua, Rahab, Achan, Phinehas, Eleazar, Caleb

Book profile:
Number of chapters: 24
Number of verses: 658
Average reading time: 1 hour, 37 minutes

What to look for:
- Jesus Christ as the Commander of the Lord's Army (5:14-15)
- spiritual evidence that Joshua was well equipped to replace Moses as the leader of Israel
- evidence that continued possession of the land was conditioned on obedience to God and that failure to obey brought failure to conquer their enemies

Why you should read Joshua:
Most people define success in terms of money or power. But God defines it much differently. Joshua helps us to understand that God's work, done in God's way, will bring God's success. This book will adjust your thinking about success.

Judges
The Book of Repeated Failures

Written:
Author: probably Samuel
Audience: the people of Israel
Date: 1050–1000 B.C.

Overview:
Subject: Israel's failure to drive out the residents of the Promised Land results in repeated regressions into sin
Scope: the events of Judges span about 550 years, from the death of Joshua to the civil war against the Benjamites
Setting: the land of Canaan; once the Jewish people were established in this land it became known as Israel

Three keys:
Key chapters: 2 (Israel's repeated cycles of apostasy begin); 6–8 (Gideon's story); 13–16 (Samson's story)
Key verses: 6:36-40; 7:7-8; 11:30-31; 16:19, 30; 17:6; 21:25
Key people: Othniel, Ehud, Deborah, Barak, Gideon, Abimelech, Jephthah, Samson, Delilah

Book profile:
Number of chapters: 21
Number of verses: 618
Average reading time: 1 hour, 35 minutes

What to look for:
- Jesus Christ as the Messenger of Jehovah (13:8, 17-21)
- evidence that God delights in bringing strength out of our human weaknesses, as is seen in the stories of Gideon, Barak, Samson, and others
- multiple examples of God using the unconventional, such as the left-handed Ehud, Shamgar's oxgoad, Jael's tent stake, and Samson's jawbone

Why you should read Judges:
Anything we value more than we value God will become our god. Break the cycle of defeat by learning from Israel, whose spiritual decay led the people to political defeat because they valued their freedom to sin more highly than they valued purity before the God of heaven.

Ruth
The Book of the Kinsman Redeemer

Written:
Author: perhaps Samuel
Audience: the people of Israel
Date: 1011–970 B.C.

Overview:
Subject: God sovereignly brings together two people who are key characters in the lineage of Jesus the Messiah
Scope: the events of Ruth cover about twelve years
Setting: Moab, the land east of the Dead Sea, and Bethlehem in Israel

Three keys:
Key chapters: 1 (Ruth's decision to stick with Naomi); 4 (Boaz becomes kinsman redeemer to Ruth)
Key verses: 1:16-17; 2:20; 3:11; 4:9-10, 13, 17
Key people: Ruth, Naomi, Boaz, Elimelech, Mahlon, Chilion

Book profile:
Number of chapters: 4
Number of verses: 85
Average reading time: 14 minutes

What to look for:
- Jesus Christ as the Kinsman Redeemer (4:14)
- a romance story of a Gentile woman who married a Jewish man (the only other book of the Bible named for a woman, Esther, is the story of a Jewish woman who married a Gentile man)
- the roots of the Messianic family, the ancestors of Jesus Christ

Why you should read Ruth:
Be encouraged—integrity is rewarded. The story of Ruth is the story of three people who remained true to God and maintained their integrity in the face of a society that was coming apart at the seams. If these three can maintain their integrity, so can we.

First Samuel

The Book of Prophets and Kings

Written:
Authors: Samuel and others
Audience: the people of Israel
Date: 1000 B.C.

Overview:
Subject: God relates to His people through Samuel, the prophet and judge, and through Israel's first kings—Saul and David
Scope: the events of 1 Samuel span about 115 years, from the birth of Samuel to the death of King Saul
Setting: the land of Israel

Three keys:
Key chapters: 1 (the birth of Samuel); 8 (Israel demands a king); 10 (Saul anointed king); 16 (David anointed king); 17 (David and Goliath)
Key verses: 1:26-28; 2:2; 6:20; 8:4-7; 12:24; 13:14; 15:22; 16:7; 17:45, 47, 49, 51; 26:11
Key people: Eli, Hannah, Samuel, Saul, Jonathan, David, Nabal, Abigail

Book profile:
Number of chapters: 31
Number of verses: 810
Average reading time: 2 hours, 23 minutes

What to look for:
- Jesus Christ as the Man after God's Own Heart (13:14)
- stories of notable contrasts—Samuel and Saul, David and Goliath, Abigail and Nabal—and how each fared with God
- the transition from a theocracy (a kingdom ruled by God) to a monarchy (a kingdom ruled by one king) and the changes that result

Why you should read 1 Samuel:
Learn to make right choices. This book is filled with spiritual champions and spiritual chumps. When you need to know what it takes to be a champion for God, look to people like Hannah, Samuel, and David. If chump is your choice, look to Saul, Hophni, and Phinehas. And remember, even champions can become chumps when they sin against God.

Second Samuel
The Book of David's Reign

Written:
Author: Samuel? Ezra or Jeremiah?
Audience: the people of Israel
Date: 1000 B.C.

Overview:
Subject: the years of David's reign are marked by national victory and personal defeat
Scope: the events of 2 Samuel cover about forty years, from the death of Saul to near the end of David's reign
Setting: the land of Israel

Three keys:
Key chapters: 5 (David becomes Israel's second king); 11 (David's sin with Bathsheba); 15 (Absalom's rebellion)
Key verses: 1:27; 5:12; 7:12-13; 11:1-5; 12:7; 22:47; 24:24
Key people: David, Bathsheba, Nathan, Joab, Absalom, Ittai, Hushai

Book profile:
Number of chapters: 24
Number of verses: 695
Average reading time: 1 hour, 48 minutes

What to look for:
- Jesus Christ as the Seed of David (7:12-13)
- the loyalty and disloyalty of David's friends and family
- mistakes that David made that prove he was his own worst enemy

Why you should read 2 Samuel:
Watch out for good times. Sin is a dirty business. Learn from David that often you plummet into the depths of your greatest sin immediately after rising to the heights of your greatest victory. It's when things are going well that we must be especially vigilant against temptation. Be on guard. If you seem to be breezing along in your faith, a tornado may be ahead.

First Kings
The Book of the Divided Kingdom

Written:
Author: possibly Jeremiah or Ezra
Audience: the people of Israel and Judah
Date: 560–536 B.C.

Overview:
Subject: God relates to His chosen people through King Solomon and the kings who follow after the kingdom is divided
Scope: the events of 1 Kings span about 120 years, from the close of David's reign to the death of King Jehoshaphat of Judah
Setting: the land of Israel, now divided into ten kingdoms in the north and two in the south

Three keys:
Key chapters: 3 (Solomon's wisdom); 12 (the kingdom divides); 18 (Elijah and the God who answers by fire)
Key verses: 3:9; 9:4-5; 11:11, 36; 12:16; 18:21, 24; 19:11-12
Key people: David, Solomon, Rehoboam, Jeroboam, Elijah, Ahab, Jezebel

Book profile:
Number of chapters: 22
Number of verses: 816
Average reading time: 1 hour, 7 minutes

What to look for:
- Jesus Christ as the Still, Small Voice of God (19:12)
- examples of God rewarding loyalty and punishing apostasy
- the division and decay of the kingdom

Why you should read 1 Kings:
False gods change names and clothes, but they do not, indeed cannot, change what they are. They are pathetic thieves, robbing of real intimacy with the one true God all those who pay them the slightest homage. Make the choice for yourself. If Jesus is God, follow Him. If not, follow somebody else. But make up your mind and get off the fence.

Second Kings
The Book of the Fallen Kingdoms

Written:
Author: possibly Jeremiah or Ezra
Audience: the people of Israel and Judah
Date: 560–536 B.C.

Overview:
Subject: the collapse of the Jewish kingdom; apostasy becomes complete and God's judgment is certain
Scope: the events of 2 Kings cover about three hundred years, from the death of Ahab to the end of Jehoiachin's reign
Setting: the land of Israel, now divided into ten kingdoms in the north and two in the south

Three keys:
Key chapters: 2 (Elijah's ministry ends; Elisha's begins); 18 (the fall of Samaria); 19 (Hezekiah's prayer); 22 (Josiah's reforms); 24–25 (the fall of Jerusalem)
Key verses: 2:9; 18:10-12; 21:13; 22:8; 23:27; 24:10, 13-15
Key people: Elijah, Elisha, Jezebel, Jehu, Hezekiah, Hoshea, Sennacherib, Isaiah, Manasseh, Josiah, Jehoiachin, Jehoiakim, Zedekiah, Nebuchadnezzar

Book profile:
Number of chapters: 25
Number of verses: 719
Average reading time: 1 hour, 55 minutes

What to look for:
- Jesus Christ as the King of Kings (23:25)
- the many miracles and revivals that shaped Hebrew history
- the rise of prophecy and the prophetic office coinciding with the decline of human leadership and the kingly office

Why you should read 2 Kings:
Reading of God's miraculous interventions in Israel's and Judah's histories encourages us to believe that God can do it again. As Elisha did, ask God for a double portion to be a strong force against the darkness of this sinful age. Like Elijah, Elisha, Isaiah, and others, believe that God can use you, that He wants to use you in an expanded and enlarged way.

First Chronicles
The Book of Israel's Genealogy

Written:
Author: Ezra
Audience: the people of Israel and Judah
Date: 450–400 B.C.

Overview:
Subject: confining itself mainly to the kingdom of Judah, the Chronicles provide a good commentary on historical events not recorded in the books of Samuel and Kings
Scope: the events of 1 Chronicles cover about forty years
Setting: the land of Israel

Three keys:
Key chapters: 4 (the prayer of Jabez); 17 (David forbidden to build the temple); 21 (David sins in numbering the people); 28 (David encourages Solomon)
Key verses: 4:9-10; 14:2; 16:22; 17:11-14; 21:7, 13; 28:9, 20
Key people: David, Solomon, Joab

Book profile:
Number of chapters: 29
Number of verses: 942
Average reading time: 1 hour, 54 minutes

What to look for:
- Jesus Christ as the One Who Searches Our Hearts (28:9)
- unique differences between the account of 1 Chronicles and the similar events recorded in 1 and 2 Samuel
- evidence that Ezra is refreshing the minds of the new generation returning from Babylonian captivity about the genealogy of David and the promise of Israel's future great king, David's greater Son, Jesus

Why you should read 1 Chronicles:
Praise God anytime! Use 1 Chronicles to remind yourself that thankfulness to God is always appropriate, but it is essential immediately after God shows His goodness in your life. David's psalm of thanksgiving came after the ark of God found its rightful place. When God is in His rightful place in our lives, thanksgiving will follow.

Second Chronicles
The Book of Jewish History

Written:
Author: Ezra
Audience: the people of Israel and Judah
Date: 430–400 B.C.

Overview:
Subject: God graciously deals with His people, from the building of Solomon's temple to the invasion by the Babylonian king Nebuchadnezzar
Scope: the events of 2 Chronicles span about 450 years
Setting: the land of Judah

Three keys:
Key chapters: 7 (the Lord appears to Solomon); 20 (Jehoshaphat's faith in God); 34 (Josiah's reforms); 36 (the fall of Jerusalem)
Key verses: 7:14; 13:18; 15:7; 16:9; 20:15, 17; 25:9; 36:19-21
Key people: Solomon, the queen of Sheba, Rehoboam, Asa, Jehoshaphat, Jehoram, Joash, Uzziah, Ahaz, Hezekiah, Manasseh, Josiah

Book profile:
Number of chapters: 36
Number of verses: 822
Average reading time: 2 hours, 22 minutes

What to look for:
- Jesus Christ as the God Who Would Dwell on Earth (6:18)
- unique differences between the account of 2 Chronicles and the similar events recorded in 1 and 2 Kings
- evidence that the Lord is just as faithful and compassionate to His children in chastising them as He is in blessing them (Heb. 12:6-13)

Why you should read 2 Chronicles:
For anyone needing personal revival, 2 Chronicles is like a revival handbook. Use what you learn from the revivals under Asa, Hezekiah, and Josiah to bring revival to your own life, and then let God use your life to bring revival to your church and your nation.

Ezra
The Book of Remnant Return

Written:
Author: Ezra
Audience: the people of Israel
Date: 456–450 B.C..

Overview:
Subject: the restoration of the temple and of temple worship
Scope: the events of Ezra cover a period of about seven and a half years
Setting: Persia and Jerusalem

Three keys:
Key chapters: 1 (Cyrus' decree); 6 (dedication of the temple)
Key verses: 1:3; 6:14, 21-22; 7:10, 28; 8:31; 9:2
Key people: Cyrus, Zerubbabel, Haggai, Zechariah, Darius, Artaxerxes I, Ezra

Book profile:
Number of chapters: 10
Number of verses: 280
Average reading time: 39 minutes

What to look for:
- Jesus Christ as Lord of Heaven and Earth (5:11)
- the spiritual history of Israel as opposed to its political history
- two specific periods of recorded history: the sixth chapter ends with the restoration of the temple, while chapter seven begins with events in Ezra's life about sixty years later

Why you should read Ezra:
If you have a friend or family member who has wandered far from God and now has come back to Him, remember that much in his or her life will need to be repaired. There will be a lot of hurt and damage. Be helpful, not critical, and you will prove yourself to be an ally in his or her recovery from backsliding.

Nehemiah
The Book of Rebuilding Jerusalem's Wall

Written:
Author: Nehemiah
Audience: the people of Israel
Date: 430 B.C.

Overview:
Subject: Nehemiah shows the fulfillment of the prophecies of Zechariah and Daniel concerning the rebuilding of Jerusalem's wall
Scope: the events of Nehemiah cover about fifteen years
Setting: Shushan, Persia's capital, and Jerusalem, Judah's capital

Three keys:
Key chapters: 1–2 (Nehemiah prays and prepares for service); 8 (the people read God's Word); 9 (the people reaffirm their loyalty to the covenant)
Key verses: 1:1-4, 11; 2:8; 4:6; 6:15-16; 8:8, 10; 9:17
Key people: Nehemiah, Ezra, Sanballat, Tobiah, Geshem

Book profile:
Number of chapters: 13
Number of verses: 406
Average reading time: 1 hour

What to look for:
- Jesus Christ as the Joy of the Lord (8:10)
- evidence of Nehemiah's leadership skills in difficult situations
- the personal character qualities of Nehemiah, such as humility, holiness, and obedience, that made him useful to God

Why you should read Nehemiah:
Let the story of Nehemiah encourage you. If you are right before God, He can use you mightily even if it doesn't seem likely to anyone else. When someone has clean hands and a pure heart and friends who have a mind to work, Satan had better look out! God is going to do something special. Ask Him to make that someone you.

Esther
The Book of God's Providential Care

Written:
Author: unknown
Audience: the Jews living in Persia
Date: 464–424 B.C.

Overview:
Subject: this book is the "Romans 8:28" of the Old Testament—God uses the young princess Esther to rescue her people from certain annihilation
Scope: the events of Esther span about twelve years
Setting: Shushan (Susa), the capital of Persia

Three keys:
Key chapters: 2 (Esther becomes queen); 6 (Mordecai is honored for his integrity); 7 (Haman is hanged); 8 (the decree from King Ahasuerus); 9 (Purim established)
Key verses: 2:16-17; 3:1-2; 4:14, 16; 7:10; 8:7-8; 9:21-22
Key people: Esther, Mordecai, King Ahasuerus (Xerxes I), Haman

Book profile:
Number of chapters: 10
Number of verses: 167
Average reading time: 32 minutes

What to look for:
- Jesus Christ as the God Above Time (4:14)
- the roots of one of modern Jewry's favorite festivals, the Feast of Purim
- the deliverance of the Jews from annihilation

Why you should read Esther:
Is it possible God has prepared you, brought you to this point in your life, to use you in a special service for Him? Consider where you have been, what God has put into you, and how you may be uniquely qualified to be used. Let the Book of Esther assure you that God prepares us for service long before He calls us and opens the door. How has He been preparing you?

Job
The Book of Suffering and Patience

Written:
Author: unknown
Audience: everyone
Date: 2100–1900 B.C.

Overview:
Subject: Job's faith in God in the midst of incredible suffering
Scope: uncertain
Setting: the land of Uz, probably located northeast of Palestine between Damascus and the Euphrates River

Three keys:
Key chapters: 1 (Job's life falls apart); 19 (Job's faith chapter); 38 (Job's appreciation of God); 42 (Job's deliverance)
Key verses: 1:1, 21; 2:3; 5:7; 13:15; 19:25-27; 23:10; 31:1; 37:23-24
Key people: Job, Eliphaz, Bildad, Zophar, Elihu

Book profile:
Number of chapters: 42
Number of verses: 1,070
Average reading time: 1 hour, 47 minutes

What to look for:
- Jesus Christ as Our Risen Redeemer (19:25-27)
- insights into the human condition in the way that others treated Job and the way he responded to that treatment
- the willingness of God to allow Job to suffer in order to ultimately bless him

Why you should read Job:
Faith is better than frustration. Have the difficulties you encountered in life destroyed your faith in God and your future? Let Job be an example to you of unshakable faith. You don't have to understand what's happening to you to hold fast to your faith; you only need to trust that God is holding fast to you.

Psalms

The Book of Poetry and Praise

Written:
Authors: David (seventy-three psalms), Asaph (twelve), the Sons of Korah (nine), Solomon (two), Heman (one), Ethan (one), Moses (one), anonymous (fifty-one)
Audience: the people of Israel
Date: 1440–400 B.C.

Overview:
Subject: God's dealings with His people and their worship and praise
Scope: the events of Psalms span about two thousand years, from Moses (ca. 1475 B.C.) to the days after Israel's return from captivity
Setting: the Holy Land

Three keys:
Key chapters: 1 (the two ways); 19 (the glory of God); 22 (the Suffering Messiah); 23 (the Good Shepherd); 37 (trust and obedience); 42 (thirsting for God); 51 (David's confession of sin); 91 (the secret place); 100 (gladness and thanksgiving); 119 (the Word of God); 139 (fearfully and wonderfully made); 150 (the pinnacle of praise)
Key verses: 19:14; 23:4; 24:3-4; 27:1; 30:5; 33:12; 42:1; 46:10; 66:18; 73:25; 84:10; 86:5; 89:1; 91:1; 101:2-3; 103:1; 116:15; 118:24; 119:11, 89, 105, 130; 121:1-2; 122:6; 126:5-6; 127:3; 130:3; 133:1; 138:2; 139:23-24; 145:18; 150:6
Key people: David, Asaph, sons of Korah, Solomon, Heman, Ethan, Moses

Book profile:
Number of chapters: 150 psalms
Number of verses: 2,461
Average reading time: 3 hours, 50 minutes

What to look for:
- Jesus Christ as Our Shepherd (23:1) and Secret Place (91:1)
- a way to read the psalms, with a certain cadence, that helps you to appreciate that these are pieces of lyric poetry
- how often the psalms seem to begin in doubt and despair but end in faith and hope

Why you should read the Psalms:

A.C. Gaebelein used to say, "A psalm a day keeps worry away." Use the psalms to lift your spirit, to direct your praise, to appreciate God's care and compassion for you. If you need your spirit lifted daily, read a psalm a day.

Proverbs
The Book of God's Wisdom

Written:
Authors: Solomon, Agur, King Lemuel
Audience: Solomon's son and, by extension, all Israel
Date: 971–931 B.C.

Overview:
Subject: a collection of succinct sayings about life and paternal counsel about living God's way
Scope: uncertain
Setting: the land of Israel

Three keys:
Key chapters: 2 (the search for and source of wisdom); 8 (the value of practical wisdom); 31 (the godly woman)
Key verses: 1:7; 3:5-6; 4:5; 9:10; 11:14, 30; 14:34; 15:3; 16:25; 18:24; 22:6; 24:10, 16; 27:1; 28:13; 30:5; 31:10, 28
Key people: Solomon, Agur, Lemuel

Book profile:
Number of chapters: 31
Number of verses: 915
Average reading time: 1 hour, 27 minutes

What to look for:
- Jesus Christ as the Wisdom of God (4:5-8)
- clever wording that helps you remember the wisdom you learn from these proverbs
- words of wisdom about the practical issues of life

Why you should read Proverbs:
Almost every issue of life is addressed in Proverbs—including how to manage your money, how to get along with relatives, how to revere God, and how to raise your children. Use the Proverbs as God's guide to the choices you must make in life. Pattern those choices after what you read in the Proverbs, and you'll make right choices every time.

Ecclesiastes
The Book of Meaningful Living

Written:
Author: Solomon
Audience: Solomon's subjects, the people of Israel
Date: 930 B.C.

Overview:
Subject: this book is designed to expose the vanity of all that is not eternal and to show that God's wisdom is superior to human wisdom
Scope: uncertain
Setting: Jerusalem

Three keys:
Key chapters: 3 (a time for everything under heaven); 5 (the source of wealth); 12 (a call to remember God)
Key verses: 2:24; 3:11; 5:19-20; 9:10; 11:1; 12:1, 13-14
Key person: Solomon

Book profile:
Number of chapters: 12
Number of verses: 222
Average reading time: 28 minutes

What to look for:
- Jesus Christ as the One Who Makes All Things Beautiful (3:11)
- reminders that all human reasoning "under the sun" is flawed and does not bring eternal benefits
- the many subjects addressed in Ecclesiastes that are also addressed by Jesus in His discourses, and the similarities in both treatments

Why you should read Ecclesiastes:
Reading this book will help you focus on eternal things and keep you from wasting your time with meaningless things. Your life can have eternal consequences, or it can simply pander after temporal needs. Choose the eternal. It lasts forever.

Song of Solomon
The Book of the Beloved

Written:
Author: Solomon
Audience: the Shulamite woman
Date: 971–931 B.C.

Overview:
Subject: the sacredness of love and sex as ordained by God within the bonds of marriage
Scope: uncertain
Setting: the Shulamite woman's garden and the king's palace in Jerusalem

Three keys:
Key chapter: 1 (the story of the bride and groom)
Key verses: 1:14-15; 2:4, 15; 5:16; 6:3; 7:10; 8:7
Key people: King Solomon, the Shulamite woman, the woman's brothers, and the young women of Jerusalem

Book profile:
Number of chapters: 8
Number of verses: 117
Average reading time: 14 minutes

What to look for:
- Jesus Christ as the Rose of Sharon and the Lily of the Valley (2:1), the Chief Among Ten Thousand (5:10), the Altogether Lovely One (5:16)
- expressions of the sacredness of love and sex as ordained by God for married couples
- the author's fondness for nature, flocks, vineyards, and the pastoral life

Why you should read Song of Solomon:
Use the Song of Solomon, God's love manual, to find new and refreshing ways to love your spouse. Use the book to be reminded of the sanctity of marriage. And use it to increase your affection for God. This song is no mere erotic poem; it expresses the way love should be between married couples and proves that God is still interested in our being completely fulfilled within the bonds of marriage.

Isaiah
The Book of Israel's Messiah

Written:
Author: Isaiah
Audience: the people of Israel
Date: 740–681 B.C.

Overview:
Subject: God's salvation of Israel and other nations through Israel's Holy One
Scope: the prophetic ministry of Isaiah covers a period of about sixty-five years, from approximately twenty-five years before the Assyrian captivity of the northern kingdom to about forty years after it
Setting: Jerusalem

Three keys:
Key chapters: 6 (Isaiah's vision of God); 7 (God's sign of victory); 9 (God's promise of peace); 14 (the fall of Lucifer); 53 (the Suffering Servant)
Key verses: 1:18; 5:20; 7:14; 9:6-7; 11:1; 14:12-15; 26:3; 30:15, 21; 40:8, 31; 44:6; 45:21-23; 52:7; 53:5-6; 55:1, 6, 8-9; 59:1-2; 64:6
Key people: Isaiah, Hezekiah, Sennacherib, Rabshakeh

Book profile:
Number of chapters: 66
Number of verses: 1,292
Average reading time: 3 hours, 24 minutes

What to look for:
- Jesus Christ as the Suffering Servant (53:2-7)
- references from Isaiah that you can identify in the New Testament
- a dramatic change in tone beginning with chapter 40; chapters 1–39 are a prelude to the joy of chapters 40–66

Why you should read Isaiah:
When someone wants to know if God saves in the Old Testament the same way He saves in the New, point them to Isaiah. The word *salvation* is mentioned at least twenty-eight times. Isaiah points forward to the event that brings salvation, the cross of Calvary, just as the New Testament largely points back to that event. Faith in God's promises has always been the way God saves, whether those promises are found in Isaiah 53, John 3, or anywhere else in Scripture.

Jeremiah
The Book of Warning and Judgment

Written:
Author: Jeremiah
Audience: the people of Judah, the southern kingdom
Date: 627–586 B.C.

Overview:
Subject: God's message concerning the sins of Judah in general and Jerusalem in particular, and the judgment of God as a result
Scope: the prophetic ministry of Jeremiah covers about forty years
Setting: Jerusalem

Three keys:
Key chapters: 1 (the call of Jeremiah); 2 (Jeremiah's plea for the Jews to return to God); 18 (the second-chance God); 31 (God's love in the midst of judgment)
Key verses: 1:5; 2:19; 7:23-24; 8:20; 9:23-24; 15:16; 17:9; 18:1-4; 23:29; 24:7; 29:11; 31:3, 34; 32:27; 33:3; 37:17
Key people: Jeremiah, Baruch, Judah's kings, King Nebuchadnezzar

Book profile:
Number of chapters: 52
Number of verses: 1,364
Average reading time: 3 hours, 44 minutes

What to look for:
- Jesus Christ as the Lord Our Righteousness (23:6)
- clues that reveal the reasons why Jeremiah is called "the weeping prophet"
- God's final efforts to save Jerusalem

Why you should read Jeremiah:
This book highlights a backslidden nation's refusal to accept God's punishment in order to be restored to God's favor. People and nations aren't much different. If you have wandered away from God and He seems to be chastising you, look upon that as His way of bringing you back into favor with Him, and favor means blessing. Accept whatever God has for you that brings you back to a dynamic relationship with Him.

Lamentations
The Book of Mourning Jerusalem

Written:
Author: Jeremiah
Audience: the people of Jerusalem
Date: 586–583 B.C.

Overview:
Subject: Jehovah demonstrates everlasting love for His people in the face of His chastening of the same people
Scope: uncertain
Setting: Jerusalem

Three keys:
Key chapters: 3 (Jeremiah shares in Israel's affliction)
Key verses: 1:12; 3:22-23, 31-32, 40
Key person: Jeremiah

Book profile:
Number of chapters: 5
Number of verses: 154
Average reading time: 17 minutes

What to look for:
- Jesus Christ as the God of Faithfulness (3:22-23)
- the patriotism of Jeremiah and his love for his hometown
- evidence that the Jews were neither to despise the chastening of the Lord nor to faint beneath it; God would bring pardon and deliverance

Why you should read Lamentations:
When you need to get right with God, use the tears of Lamentations to show you it is God's goodness that will lead you back to Him. Paul wrote that "the goodness of God leads you to repentance" (Rom. 2:4). If you look for the goodness of God even though He seems distant from you now, not only will you find it, but you will find your way back as well.

Ezekiel
The Book of Glory Lost and Regained

Written:
Author: Ezekiel
Audience: the Jews in Babylonian captivity and elsewhere
Date: 593–571 B.C.

Overview:
Subject: the vision of the glory of the Lord departing from the temple at the event of its destruction and the return of the Shekinah glory to God's house
Scope: the prophetic ministry of Ezekiel ranges over twenty-two years, from seven years before the destruction of Jerusalem until about fifteen years afterward
Setting: Babylon, with the Jews in captivity

Three keys:
Key chapters: 36 (the promise of a restored Israel); 37 (the valley of the dry bones); 38 (the prophecy against Gog and Magog)
Key verses: 1:16; 14:14, 16; 18:4, 20; 22:30; 33:11; 36:24-26; 37:3-5; 38:14-16; 44:2-3
Key people: Ezekiel, Ezekiel's wife, Nebuchadnezzar, the coming prince

Book profile:
Number of chapters: 48
Number of verses: 1,273
Average reading time: 3 hours, 18 minutes

What to look for:
- Jesus Christ as the Coming Prince (44:1-3)
- Ezekiel's dizzying array of visions, messages, poems, and dramas to convey his message to God's people
- the overwhelming number of times (more than sixty) God repeats, "And you will know that I am the Lord"

Why you should read Ezekiel:
Use the Book of Ezekiel to encourage your Jewish friends that God isn't finished yet with Israel. He has regathered His people in their ancient land, but they are mainly agnostic today. Nevertheless, the prophecy of Ezekiel reveals that God will rebuild the temple in Jerusalem. Take them to the Book of Revelation to understand how, why, and when.

Daniel
The Book of Kingdoms

Written:
Author: Daniel
Audience: God's captive people in Babylon
Date: 535-530 B.C.

Overview:
Subject: the Book of Daniel is half history, recording Daniel's capture and captivity, and half prophecy, concerning Gentile world rule from Nebuchadnezzar to the Antichrist
Scope: the prophetic ministry of Daniel covers about seventy-five years, from King Nebuchadnezzar of Babylon to King Cyrus and Darius of the Medes
Setting: Babylon

Three keys:
Key chapters: 1 (Jewish youth carried into captivity); 2 (Nebuchadnezzar's dream and Daniel's interpretation); 3 (the fiery furnace); 5 (handwriting on Belshazzar's wall); 6 (Daniel in the lions' den); 9 (Daniel's prophecy of the seventy weeks)
Key verses: 1:8; 2:20-22, 28, 47; 3:24-25; 5:27; 6:25-27; 9:24-27
Key people: Daniel, Shadrach, Meshach, Abednego, Nebuchadnezzar, Belshazzar, Darius

Book profile:
Number of chapters: 12
Number of verses: 356
Average reading time: 1 hour, 14 minutes

What to look for:
- Jesus Christ as the Fourth Man in the Fire (3:25)
- the power brokers and the flow of power from one ruler to another while God remains in control
- the dramatic change from history to prophecy in the middle of the book

Why you should read Daniel:
Daniel is the key that unlocks much of what you read in Revelation. Many New Testament prophetic references come from Daniel, such as the abomination of desolation (Matt. 24:15) and names written in a book (Rev. 13:8). When interpreting prophetic passages in the New Testament, especially Revelation, keep Daniel handy.

Hosea
The Book of Redeeming Love

Written:
Author: Hosea
Audience: the Jewish people of the northern kingdom
Date: 715 B.C.

Overview:
Subject: the apostasy of Israel and the prophecy of coming home to God's love
Scope: the prophetic ministry of Hosea spans about forty-one years, from 755 to 714 B.C.
Setting: Israel

Three keys:
Key chapters: 4 (Israel abandons her knowledge of God); 14 (God's undying love for His backslidden people)
Key verses: 1:2; 3:1; 4:6; 8:14; 10:12; 11:7-9; 14:4-5, 9
Key people: Hosea, Gomer, their children

Book profile:
Number of chapters: 14
Number of verses: 197
Average reading time: 28 minutes

What to look for:
- Jesus Christ as the Lover of Backsliders (14:4)
- God's great desire to restore us to His unfailing love
- comparisons of the images of marital infidelity between Gomer and Hosea and spiritual infidelity between Israel and God

Why you should read Hosea:
This is the backslider's book. If you or friends or family have drifted far from God, be encouraged through the story of Hosea. God knew Gomer would be unfaithful to Hosea long before they were married; still, He encouraged the marriage because He knew Gomer's sin was no match for His unfailing love. This is the perfect book for anyone who needs to know that no sin is so great that God's forgiving love is not greater still.

Joel
The Book of God's Severity and Goodness

Written:
Author: Joel
Audience: the Jews of Judah, the southern kingdom
Date: 835–796 B.C.

Overview:
Subject: Joel used the event of a devastating scourge of locusts both to call Judah to repentance and to depict greater judgment to come
Scope: the prophetic ministry of Joel covers about thirty-nine years
Setting: Jerusalem

Three keys:
Key chapter: 2 (the Day of the Lord)
Key verses: 2:12-14, 27-29, 32; 3:17
Key person: Joel

Book profile:
Number of chapters: 3
Number of verses: 73
Average reading time: 10 minutes

What to look for:
- Jesus Christ as the Outpourer of the Spirit (2:28)
- Joel's diverse literary style; he uses metaphors, similes, alliteration, parallelism, and more to paint a vivid prophecy
- the seriousness with which Joel treats the subject of his prophecy and his repeated call for a solemn assembly for the nation to repent of its sins and return to God

Why you should read Joel:
God is the ultimate Promise Keeper. Every promise of God has been fulfilled, is being fulfilled, or one day will be fulfilled. Let the Book of Joel convince you of that. Joel promised that one day in the distant future God would pour out His Spirit (2:28), and that's exactly what happened at the day of Pentecost (Acts 2). It took more than eight hundred years, but that's nothing to God. He keeps His promises no matter how long it takes.

Amos
The Book of Judgment on Sin

Written:
Author: Amos
Audience: the Jews of Israel, the northern kingdom
Date: 760 B.C.

Overview:
Subject: God's sure judgment upon Israel, Judah, and the nations around them, but with hope for forgiveness and restoration if they repent and seek the Lord
Scope: the prophetic ministry of Amos covers a period of nine years, from 764 to 755 B.C. His prophecy began two years before a tremendous earthquake, mentioned by Josephus as occurring the year King Uzziah was struck with leprosy, and so severe that it was remembered two hundred years later by Zechariah (Zech. 14:5).
Setting: Israel

Three keys:
Key chapters: 1 (the call of Amos); 9 (Israel's dispersion and restoration)
Key verses: 3:1-3; 5:24; 7:7-9, 14; 8:11; 9:13
Key people: Amos, Amaziah, Jeroboam II

Book profile:
Number of chapters: 9
Number of verses: 146
Average reading time: 22 minutes

What to look for:
- Jesus Christ as the Living Word of God (8:11)
- the unflinching commitment of Amos to deliver God's message of judgment even though it was terribly unpopular
- the theme of injustice

Why you should read Amos:
Use the Book of Amos as a reminder that sin separates us from God and that sin must be judged and forgiven before fellowship with God can be restored (1 John 1:9). If you are not enjoying the intimate fellowship with God that you desire, don't blame God. Look for unconfessed sin that would keep you from that kind of a relationship.

Obadiah

The Book of Anti-Semite Doom

Written:
Author: Obadiah
Audience: the Edomites and the Jews in Judah
Date: 848–841 B.C.

Overview:
Subject: God takes special care of His chosen people and predicts certain punishment for those who persecute them
Scope: the prophetic ministry of Obadiah's prophecy covers seven years
Setting: Judah, the southern kingdom

Three keys:
Key chapter: 1 (the reward of unrighteousness)
Key verses: 1:3-4, 10, 12, 15, 17, 21
Key people: Obadiah, the Edomites

Book profile:
Number of chapters: 1
Number of verses: 21
Average reading time: 4 minutes

What to look for:
- Jesus Christ as the Lord of His Kingdom (v. 21)
- the brevity (it's the shortest book in the Old Testament) and directness of Obadiah's prophecy against the Edomites
- the bad news for Edom contrasted with the good news for Israel

Why you should read Obadiah:
Obadiah is the story of what happens when we hold a grudge. The Edomites, descendants of Esau, never could bring themselves to forgive the Israelites, descendants of Jacob, for their ancestor's being swindled out of his birthright. Use this book to help yourself and others realize that bitterness always hurts the one who is bitter more than the one against whom a grudge is held.

Jonah
The Book of God's Mercy

Written:
Author: Jonah
Audience: the people of God
Date: 793—753 B.C.

Overview:
Subject: God's dealing with a disobedient prophet and a repentant pagan people
Scope: the prophetic ministry of Jonah happened during the reign of King Jeroboam II of Israel, which lasted forty-one years
Setting: Joppa, the Mediterranean Sea, Nineveh

Three keys:
Key chapters: 1 (Jonah's call and disobedience); 2 (Jonah's prayer); 3 (God gives Jonah a second chance); 4 (Jonah's bitterness at God's grace)
Key verses: 1:1-3, 17; 2:9; 3:1-2, 5; 4:2, 11
Key people: Jonah, the boat's captain and crew, the Ninevites

Book profile:
Number of chapters: 4
Number of verses: 48
Average reading time: 7 minutes

What to look for:
- Jesus Christ as the God of the Second Chance (3:1)
- the contrast between the generous grace of God in saving the repentant Ninevites and Jonah's ungenerous reaction to that grace
- evidence from the great wind, the great fish, the gourd, the sun, etc., that God controls His creation and uses it as He wills

Why you should read Jonah:
Have you blown it? Did you make such a big mess of things that you think God can never use you again? Read Jonah. God is the God of the second chance. When Jonah genuinely repented of his sin, God came to him a second time and recommissioned him for service. He'll do the same for you.

Micah
The Book of Doom

Written:
Author: Micah
Audience: the people of Israel and Judah
Date: 740–687 B.C.

Overview:
Subject: Micah declares Israel's sin and God's grace in bringing salvation out of certain doom
Scope: the prophetic ministry of Micah spans about forty-two years
Setting: Judah and Israel

Three keys:
Key chapters: 5 (Bethlehem prophecy); 6 (the failure of God's people to meet God's requirements); 7 (Israel's confession and intercession)
Key verses: 5:2; 6:8, 14-15; 7:18
Key people: Micah, the people of Jerusalem and Samaria

Book profile:
Number of chapters: 7
Number of verses: 105
Average reading time: 15 minutes

What to look for:
- Jesus Christ as the Bethlehemite (5:2)
- the disparity between the rich and the poor in Micah's society and how that inequity impacts his prophecy
- the prophecies of Micah seem to be mixed up: one moment he is talking about the present, the next about the future; he often repeats himself and uses incomplete sentences

Why you should read Micah:
Learn from Micah that there is nobody like God. Theologians use big words to describe God's unique qualities, such as transcendence and omnipresence, but Micah is struck with something much more personal—God's forgiveness (7:18). There is just no God like this God. Read the book and let your mouth fall open in awe at a holy God who still delights in mercy. That's the kind of God you can appreciate and get to know.

Nahum
The Book of Nineveh's Doom

Written:
Author: Nahum
Audience: the people of Nineveh and Judah
Date: 663–654 B.C.

Overview:
Subject: the sure and final judgment on stubborn Nineveh and the revelation of the majesty of God
Scope: the prophetic ministry of Nahum covers about twenty-eight years
Setting: Judah

Three keys:
Key chapters: 1 (the principles governing divine judgment); 3 (Nineveh reaps judgment)
Key verses: 1:6-9, 15; 3:5-7, 18
Key people: Nahum, the Ninevites

Book profile:
Number of chapters: 3
Number of verses: 47
Average reading time: 6 minutes

What to look for:
- Jesus Christ as the One Who Brings Good Tidings (1:15)
- the contrast between the repentant Ninevites of Jonah's prophecy and the regressive Ninevites of Nahum's prophecy
- a message of doom one hundred years after Nineveh repented under the preaching of Jonah; sometimes repentance doesn't stick

Why you should read Nahum:
Salvation cannot be transferred from one generation to another. The Ninevites repented of sin in Jonah's day, but their descendants needed a good dose of repentance in Nahum's day. If you or a friend feel you will get to heaven because your mother and father went to church, read the story of Nahum carefully. Repentance and faith are private matters. Each of us must trust Christ as Savior for ourselves. You can't go to heaven on your parents' faith.

Habakkuk
The Book of a Gracious God

Written:
Author: Habakkuk
Audience: the people of Judah, the southern kingdom
Date: 605 B.C.

Overview:
Subject: this book records the story of God's holiness as shown through His judgments upon Judah at the hands of the Chaldeans
Scope: the prophetic ministry of Habakkuk covers about fifteen years
Setting: Judah

Three keys:
Key chapters: 2 (the just shall live by faith); 3 (Habakkuk's prayer)
Key verses: 2:4, 20; 3:2, 17-19
Key people: Habakkuk, the Chaldeans

Book profile:
Number of chapters: 3
Number of verses: 56
Average reading time: 7 minutes

What to look for:
- Jesus Christ as the Lord in His Holy Temple (2:20)
- the growth of Habakkuk's faith in God as his prophecy progresses
- the effects of the invasion of Judah and the doom of the Chaldeans

Why you should read Habakkuk:
When you are prone to question God about everything, read Habakkuk. He was the "Doubting Thomas" of the Old Testament. God puts up with our questions; He even answers some of them. But as you read the Book of Habakkuk and see the prophet's faith growing, his tendency to question God diminishes. Yours should too.

Zephaniah
The Book of God's Wrath

Written:
Author: Zephaniah
Audience: Judah and all other nations
Date: 622–612 B.C.

Overview:
Subject: God's wrath on a sinful world and on Judah in particular in the Day of the Lord, and His great mercy in saving the remnant of Israel
Scope: the prophetic ministry of Zephaniah covers about nine years
Setting: Jerusalem

Three keys:
Key chapters: 1 (the day of God's wrath); 3 (God's deliverance)
Key verses: 1:14-15; 2:3; 3:14-16
Key people: Zephaniah, Josiah

Book profile:
Number of chapters: 3
Number of verses: 53
Average reading time: 6 minutes

What to look for:
- Jesus Christ as the Lord in Israel's Midst (3:15)
- the expression "the Day of the Lord"; it is used seven times
- the great wrath of God coupled with His great mercy in hiding the remnant of Israel who seek Him in the day of wrath

Why you should read Zephaniah:
Use the Book of Zephaniah to help you understand 2 Thessalonians, especially chapter two. Reading these two books together will give you a complete picture from the Old and New Testaments of what God's wrath will one day be like. We can't appreciate it now, for we know nothing but His grace. But one day the curtain of God's grace will be raised on His wrath. Many people doubt this, but God's Word says it's true, both in 2 Thessalonians and in Zephaniah.

Haggai
The Book of Temple Reconstruction

Written:
Author: Haggai
Audience: the people of Jerusalem
Date: 520 B.C.

Overview:
Subject: the need to forget self and rise up and rebuild the temple, which Nebuchadnezzer had destroyed
Scope: the prophetic ministry of Haggai covers about four months
Setting: Jerusalem

Three keys:
Key chapters: 1 (the futility of life without God); 2 (the Desire of All Nations)
Key verses: 1:4, 6, 9, 13-15; 2:7, 19
Key people: Haggai, Zerubbabel, Joshua

Book profile:
Number of chapters: 2 (only book in the Bible with just two chapters)
Number of verses: 38
Average reading time: 5 minutes

What to look for:
- Jesus Christ as the Desire of All Nations (2:7)
- the similarities between the people of God in Haggai's day and the people of God today
- the images of the futility of a life lived only for oneself and not for God

Why you should read Haggai:
Hidden within the text of Haggai is the answer to one of man's great enigmas. People are restless, anxious, even edgy. There is a universal craving for some unknown good. Foolishly, people often look for it within themselves. Some look to government. But Haggai tells you where this unknown good can be found—in the Desire of All Nations, Jesus Christ. Share the fulfillment you have found in Christ with others who are seeking good but don't know where to find it. Share the message of Haggai with them.

Zechariah
The Book of Messiah's Advent

Written:
Author: Zechariah
Audience: the Jews of Jerusalem returned from captivity
Date: 520–518 B.C.

Overview:
Subject: Zechariah was a prophet to Israel's remnant, and his ministry was to stir up the public to rebuild the temple
Scope: the prophetic ministry of Zechariah covers about two years
Setting: Jerusalem

Three keys:
Key chapters: 3 (Israel's promised restoration after judgment); 14 (the Second Coming of Christ)
Key verses: 2:8, 11; 3:8; 4:6; 6:12-13; 8:3, 7-8, 22; 9:9; 12:10; 14:1-4
Key people: Zechariah, Zerubbabel, Joshua the high priest, the Branch

Book profile:
Number of chapters: 14
Number of verses: 211
Average reading time: 29 minutes

What to look for:
- Jesus Christ as the Branch (6:12) and Coming King (9:9)
- the words of Zechariah that you recognize as quoted in the New Testament
- reassurance that God's love and purpose for His people are unchangeable and will be fulfilled

Why you should read Zechariah:
The Book of Zechariah is the story of God's people returning from captivity to their homeland to start over. If you need incentive to start over in some area of your life or your relationships with others, read Zechariah. Wade through the prophecies and symbols and get to the heart of his message—it's possible to start over, with God's grace.

Malachi
The Book of Final Rebuke

Written:
Author: Malachi
Audience: the Jews of Jerusalem
Date: 450–430 B.C.

Overview:
Subject: the prophet Malachi predicts certain judgment on God's people because they hold God in contempt
Scope: the prophetic ministry of Malachi spans about twenty years
Setting: Jerusalem

Three keys:
Key chapters: 3 (the unchanging God); 4 (the Day of the Lord and the promise of restoration)
Key verses: 2:17; 3:1-2, 6, 8; 4:1-2, 5-6
Key people: Malachi, the Sun of Righteousness, the prophet Elijah

Book profile:
Number of chapters: 4
Number of verses: 55
Average reading time: 10 minutes

What to look for:
- Jesus Christ as the Sun of Righteousness (4:2)
- Malachi's use of dialogue with the unfaithful people of God in writing his prophecy
- God's final message to the Israelites, revealing both His love for them and His holiness in judging their sins

Why you should read Malachi:
In a day when things seem to change constantly, many people are looking for something they can be sure of, something they can hold on to, someone who will not change. Malachi 3:6 says, "For I am the Lord, I do not change." If you're looking for some stability in your life, look to the changeless God.

Matthew
The Book of Christ the King

Written:
Author: Matthew
Audience: Jewish believers of the first century
Date: A.D. 50

Overview:
Subject: the birth, life, teaching, death, and resurrection of Jesus Christ
Scope: the events recorded in Matthew's Gospel cover about thirty-four years
Setting: the Holy Land—Bethlehem, Egypt, Nazareth, the Judean wilderness, Galilee, and Jerusalem

Three keys:
Key chapters: 1 (the genealogy of Jesus Christ); 5–7 (the Sermon on the Mount); 12 (the Pharisees, representing Israel, reject Jesus); 24–25 (the Olivet Discourse); 28 (Jesus' resurrection and the Great Commission)
Key verses: 1:20-21; 3:11; 4:1; 6:19-21, 33; 9:37-38; 10:32-33; 11:28; 16:16-18; 19:26; 23:37; 24:35; 25:13; 27:54; 28:6-7, 18-20
Key people: Jesus, Mary, Joseph, the wise men, John the Baptist, the disciples, the religious leaders of Jerusalem, Caiaphas, Pilate, Mary Magdalene

Book profile:
Number of chapters: 28
Number of verses: 1,071
Average reading time: 2 hours, 9 minutes

What to look for:
- Jesus Christ as the King of the Jews (2:2; 27:11)
- Matthew's repeated references to fulfilled prophecy (seventeen times)
- groupings of Jesus' teachings collected in five main places, beginning with the Sermon on the Mount

Why you should read Matthew:
Matthew doesn't hesitate to record some shady characters in Jesus' family tree in order to provide an accurate record of His ancestry through David to Abraham. That's important. It means Jesus is the legitimate heir to the throne of David, and Matthew lays out the case that Jesus is the Messiah of the people of God.

Mark
The Book of Christ the Servant

Written:
Author: Mark
Audience: the Christians in Rome, where Mark wrote his Gospel
Date: A.D. 57–60

Overview:
Subject: the life, teachings, death, resurrection, and ascension of Jesus Christ
Scope: the events recorded in Mark's Gospel cover a little more than three years
Setting: the Holy Land—the Jordan Valley, the land of the Gadarenes, Galilee, Jericho, and Jerusalem

Three keys:
Key chapters: 8 (Peter's confession of Jesus as Messiah); 16 (the resurrection of Jesus Christ and commission to go into all the world)
Key verses: 1:14, 39; 3:6; 4:13-20; 8:34-37; 10:17-22, 43-45; 16:15
Key people: Jesus, the disciples, Pilate, the Jewish religious leaders

Book profile:
Number of chapters: 16
Number of verses: 678
Average reading time: 1 hour, 21 minutes

What to look for:
- Jesus Christ as the Servant of the Lord (10:43-45)
- touches of personal and historical information that likely Mark learned from Peter
- a fast-paced life of Christ, like a script from an action movie

Why you should read Mark:
Jesus was determined to lead as a servant and to set an example for you and me. Here's His message: If you want to win, lose yourself. If you want to be first, be last. If you want to be a leader, be a servant. Greatness is not determined by how many people you lead but by how many you serve.

Luke
The Book of Christ the Perfect Man

Written:
Author: Luke
Audience: Theophilus and Gentile Christians
Date: A.D. 60

Overview:
Subject: the birth, life, teachings, death, resurrection, and ascension of Jesus Christ
Scope: the events recorded in Luke's Gospel span about thirty-four years
Setting: the Holy Land—Bethlehem, Nazareth, the Jordan Valley, the Judean wilderness, Galilee, the land of the Gadarenes, and Jerusalem

Three keys:
Key chapters: 2 (the Christmas story); 15 (the three parables); 24 (the proof of Jesus' resurrection)
Key verses: 1:3-4, 30-33; 2:8-20; 6:38; 13:5; 15:11-32; 19:10, 40; 22:54-62; 23:20-22; 24:27
Key people: Jesus, Elizabeth, Zacharias, John the Baptist, Mary, the disciples, Herod the Great, Pilate, Mary Magdalene, Cleopas

Book profile:
Number of chapters: 24
Number of verses: 1,151
Average reading time: 2 hours, 16 minutes

What to look for:
- Jesus Christ as the Son of Man (19:10)
- Luke's emphasis on Jesus' humanity as seen in the record of His personal interest in people, including the poor and outcast
- stories of humility that results in exaltation—for example, the publican, the prodigal, the Savior

Why you should read Luke:
Jesus' message to His disciples was simple: The way up is down. Whoever exalts himself will be humbled. The way to victory is surrender to the Perfect Man. Use the teaching and example of Christ Jesus and discover the secret to spiritual success. Humble yourself before God, and He will lift you up.

John

The Book of Christ the Son of God

Written:
Author: John
Audience: Christians and non-Christians of the first century
Date: A.D. 85–95

Overview:
Subject: the life, teachings, death, resurrection, and post-resurrection appearances of Jesus Christ
Scope: the events recorded in John's Gospel cover from eternity past to the post-resurrection appearance of Jesus Christ in Galilee
Setting: the Holy Land—the Jordan Valley, Galilee, Samaria, Bethany, and Jerusalem

Three keys:
Key chapters: 3 (Jesus, only-begotten of the Father, Savior of the world); 10 (the believer's relationship with Jesus Christ); 15 (abiding in Christ); 19 (the crucifixion and death of Jesus Christ)
Key verses: 1:1-3, 11-12, 29; 3:14-18, 36; 5:24; 6:66-69; 8:32, 36; 14:1-6; 17:17; 18:38; 19:16-21, 30, 38-42; 20:13-16, 30-31; 21:15-17
Key people: Jesus, John the Baptist, the disciples, Mary, Martha, Lazarus, Jesus' mother, Peter, Mary Magdalene, Joseph of Arimathea

Book profile:
Number of chapters: 21
Number of verses: 879
Average reading time: 1 hour, 54 minutes

What to look for:
- Jesus Christ as the Son of God (19:7)
- John's careful presentation of the facts so as to bring his readers to believe that Jesus is the Son of God and Savior of the world
- word pictures of who Jesus is, such as water, lamb, bread, light, shepherd, and vine

Why you should read John:

Nowhere is the gospel more clearly presented than in the Gospel of John. If you are looking for a way to share the gospel story with a friend, John has some classic passages that God's servants have used for generations, such as chapters three, five, and ten. Become familiar with these passages and you will never be a "witless witness."

Acts
The Book of the Early Church

Written:
Author: Luke
Audience: Theophilus and the first-century church
Date: A.D. 60–62

Overview:
Subject: the birth and development of the Jerusalem church and the spread of Christianity throughout the Roman world
Scope: the events of the Book of Acts cover about thirty-three years, from A.D. 30 to 63
Setting: the Holy Land and the Roman world

Three keys:
Key chapters: 2 (the birth of the church); 9 (the conversion of Saul of Tarsus); 13 (first missionary journey); 16 (the Macedonian vision); 27 (Paul's shipwreck)
Key verses: 1:8, 11; 2:14-18, 32, 42-47; 3:14-16; 4:12; 5:29; 6:1-4; 9:1-6, 20, 29-31; 10:34-36; 13:1-3; 16:9, 30-31; 17:6, 22-23; 26:19, 28
Key people: Peter, John, James, Stephen, Philip, Paul, Barnabas, Timothy, Silas, Titus, Ananias, Felix, Festus, Agrippa

Book profile:
Number of chapters: 28
Number of verses: 1,007
Average reading time: 2 hours, 33 minutes

What to look for:
- Jesus Christ as the Ascended Lord (1:9-11)
- God building His church through persecution and hardship
- words indicating phenomenal church growth, such as *added, thousand,* and *multitude*

Why you should read Acts:
The best confirmation of facts is by an eyewitness. Acts is the written record of eyewitnesses to the resurrected Lord. Give these eyewitnesses their due. They had nothing to gain by lying and everything to lose. If you are looking for the truth, let God speak to you through people who knew what they were talking about. They were there.

Romans
The Book of God's Grace

Written:
Author: Paul
Audience: the church at Rome in central Italy
Date: A.D. 57

Overview:
Subject: the universal sin of mankind and the grace of God, which provides hope for the sinner
Setting: written at Corinth as Paul was preparing for his journey to Jerusalem about issues facing the believers at Rome

Three keys:
Key chapters: 1 (man's need of salvation); 3 (the total depravity of mankind); 5 (how sin and salvation come to us); 8 (assurance of salvation); 12 (how to live the Christian life)
Key verses: 1:16-18; 3:10, 20, 23-24; 4:3; 5:1-2, 6-8; 6:23; 8:1, 16-17, 28, 38-39; 10:9, 13; 12:1-2; 14:10
Key people: Paul, Abraham, Adam, Jacob, Esau, Pharaoh, Phoebe, Tertius

Book profile:
Number of chapters: 16
Number of verses: 433
Average reading time: 1 hour, 1 minute

What to look for:
- Jesus Christ as the Lord Our Righteousness (10:4)
- the logic of the apostle in building his case for man's need of salvation and God's gracious plan of redemption
- Paul's repeated emphasis on righteousness, our lack of it, and God's provision for all who need it

Why you should read Romans:
Romans is a book to savor, to read slowly and carefully. If you do, you will discover an irrefutable argument for the need of a Savior and an irresistible grace that draws needy sinners to Him. Use the Book of Romans to strengthen your faith, guide your Christian conduct, and provide substance to your theological understanding.

First Corinthians
The Book of Spiritual Challenges

Written:
Author: Paul
Audience: the church at Corinth in southern Greece
Date: A.D. 55-56

Overview:
Subject: the spiritual immaturity of a local church and God's gifting of church members to minister to each other in unity
Setting: written at Ephesus on Paul's third missionary journey about issues facing the fledgling church at Corinth

Three keys:
Key chapters: 1 (the power of preaching the Word); 3 (examination at the judgment seat of Christ); 13 (the way of Christian love); 15 (the promise of bodily resurrection)
Key verses: 1:17-18, 23; 3:9, 11-15; 4:2; 6:19-20; 9:16, 27; 10:12-13; 11:23-30; 12:4-6; 13:1-3, 13; 15:12-20, 51-55, 57-58
Key people: Paul, Timothy, the Corinthian church, Chloe's household

Book profile:
Number of chapters: 16
Number of verses: 437
Average reading time: 1 hour, 2 minutes

What to look for:
- Jesus Christ as the Firstfruits of the Dead (15:20)
- the specific responses of Paul to the direct questions asked of him by the Corinthian believers
- a roller coaster of emotions evidenced by Paul, ranging from disappointment and rebuke to commendation and hope

Why you should read 1 Corinthians:
There is a vital relationship among all the members of Christ's Body. You have a contribution to make to others. Find out what God has given to you by way of spiritual gifts, natural abilities, and talents. Whatever He put into you, He expects to get out. You are important!

Second Corinthians
The Book of Paul's Defense

Written:
Author: Paul
Audience: the church at Corinth in southern Greece
Date: A.D. 57

Overview:
Subject: Paul defends his ministry by proving that he has served the Lord with faithfulness and integrity
Setting: written at Philippi on Paul's third missionary journey

Three keys:
Key chapters: 5 (motivation for ministry); 8–9 (God's plan for giving)
Key verses: 2:11; 3:17-18; 4:5-6; 5:9-11, 14-15, 17, 20-21; 6:14; 9:6-7, 15; 12:14-15; 13:5
Key people: Paul, Timothy, Titus, false teachers, the Corinthian church

Book profile:
Number of chapters: 13
Number of verses: 257
Average reading time: 38 minutes

What to look for:
- Jesus Christ as Our Sufficiency (3:5)
- the contentious nature of issues addressed in this epistle and Paul's deliberate responses to those issues
- insights into the apostle's life in this, the most personal of all Paul's epistles

Why you should read 2 Corinthians:
When you have to answer your critics, and someday you will, don't allow your frustration to keep you from the passion of your calling. In the most defensive of Paul's letters, he focuses on the ministry of reconciliation. Let 2 Corinthians convince you that you can defend yourself without being defensive.

Galatians
The Book of Christian Liberty

Written:
Author: Paul
Audience: the churches in southern Galatia in central Turkey
Date: A.D. 48–49

Overview:
Subject: the Christian is not to live under law but under the liberty of grace
Setting: written from Antioch after Paul's second missionary journey

Three keys:
Key chapters: 3 (justification by faith); 5 (walking by the fruit of the Spirit)
Key verses: 1:8, 15-18; 2:20; 3:11, 13, 16, 20, 22, 27-28; 4:4; 5:1, 13-14, 16, 22-25; 6:7, 14
Key people: Paul, Peter, Barnabas, Titus, Abraham, false teachers, the Galatian believers

Book profile:
Number of chapters: 6
Number of verses: 149
Average reading time: 18 minutes

What to look for:
- Jesus Christ as Our Freedom (5:1)
- Paul's true explanation of salvation as opposed to the false teaching the Galatian believers had come to embrace
- evidences that Galatians is the believers' Magna Carta, our Declaration of Independence, our statement of emancipation from the Law and freedom in the gospel

Why you should read Galatians:
When the religious Pharisees and legalists of the church heap upon you rules and regulations that are not of biblical origin, use the Book of Galatians to stand fast in your liberty in Christ Jesus. Be courteous, be gentle, be kind, but be firm in liberty. This is not freedom to sin; it is freedom to live in the benefits of Christ's death at Calvary.

Ephesians
The Book of the Church

Written:
Author: Paul
Audience: the church at Ephesus in western Turkey
Date: A.D. 60

Overview:
Subject: the calling, conduct, and conflict of the church and how church members are to pattern their lifestyle after Jesus Christ, the Head of the Church
Setting: written from Rome while Paul was in prison

Three keys:
Key chapters: 1 (the believer's position in Christ); 4 (unity in the Body); 6 (strong in His strength)
Key verses: 1:3-8, 13-14; 2:1, 8-10; 3:20-21; 4:1-6, 14-16, 30-32; 6:10-17
Key people: Paul, Tychicus, the Ephesian church

Book profile:
Number of chapters: 6
Number of verses: 155
Average reading time: 21 minutes

What to look for:
- Jesus Christ as the Head of the Church (5:23)
- Paul's emphasis on unity between the Gentile and Jewish factions of the first-century church
- the apostle's treatment of some of the greatest doctrines of the faith: grace, eternal election, and redemption by Christ's blood, among others

Why you should read Ephesians:
In the twenty-first century, with some churches displaying more entertainment than evangelism, more style than substance, and people often opting for online religious discussion rather than a live church community relationship, we need instruction on how to "do" church and why we do it. Ephesians provides what we need. It is a handbook on church philosophy and practice. It can make the difference in the quality of your church experience.

Philippians
The Book of Rejoicing

Written:
Author: Paul
Audience: the church at Philippi in northern Greece
Date: A.D. 61–62

Overview:
Subject: the apostle expresses his love and affection for the Philippians and encourages them to live a holy and humble life
Setting: written from Rome while Paul was in prison

Three keys:
Key chapter: 2 (Christ's humiliation and exaltation)
Key verses: 1:6, 21; 2:5-11; 3:10-14; 4:4, 13, 19
Key people: Paul, Timothy, Epaphroditus, Euodias, Syntyche, the Philippian church

Book profile:
Number of chapters: 4
Number of verses: 104
Average reading time: 12 minutes

What to look for:
- Jesus Christ as the Highly Exalted Lord (2:9)
- frequent references to words like *joy* and *rejoice*—used a dozen times in just four chapters
- Paul's constant focus on Christ Jesus as all we need: our life, our ideal, our power, our cause for rejoicing

Why you should read Philippians:
Have you been a little down lately? We all get that way at times. Read the Book of Philippians and find out why Paul could be sky-high even though he was in a Roman jail. Our attitudes, our joy, our outlook on life don't arise from what's around us but from what's in us.

Colossians
The Book of Christ's Preeminence

Written:
Author: Paul
Audience: the church at Colossae in central Turkey
Date: A.D. 60–62

Overview:
Subject: the fullness of Christ and our fullness in Him
Setting: written from Rome while Paul was in prison

Three keys:
Key chapters: 1 (the preeminence of Jesus Christ); 3 (how to live a holy life)
Key verses: 1:14-19; 2:3, 6-7, 9-10; 3:1-3, 5, 12, 17, 23
Key people: Paul, Tychicus, Onesimus, Aristarchus, Mark, Epaphras, the Colossian church

Book profile:
Number of chapters: 4
Number of verses: 95
Average reading time: 11 minutes

What to look for:
- Jesus Christ as the Fullness of the Godhead (2:9)
- Paul's emphasis on the glory of Jesus Christ in order to counteract those who falsely taught that Jesus was not both human and divine
- similarities and contrasts with Ephesians, which emphasizes the church, and with Philippians, where Christ empties Himself. In Colossians Christ is restored to His rightful position of preeminence as the Head of the Church.

Why you should read Colossians:
When non-Christians come to witness at your door, often two by two, you need to know who Jesus is. That question separates truth from error, the true church from the cults. Colossians can help. Use this letter to come to some conclusions about the position of Christ—not a man or an angel or a simple prophet, but God in the flesh and the Head of the Church.

First Thessalonians
The Book of Christ's Return

Written:
Author: Paul
Audience: the church at Thessalonica in northern Greece
Date: A.D. 50–51

Overview:
Subject: the coming of the Lord Jesus for His church
Setting: written from Corinth on Paul's second missionary journey

Three keys:
Key chapters: 3 (the goal of our salvation); 4 (the rapture of the church)
Key verses: 1:9-10; 2:19-20; 3:12-13; 4:3-4, 13-18; 5:2-4, 14, 16-18
Key people: Paul, Timothy, Silas, the Thessalonian church

Book profile:
Number of chapters: 5
Number of verses: 89
Average reading time: 11 minutes

What to look for:
- Jesus Christ as the Coming Lord (4:16-17)
- the personal nature of much of what Paul writes in this epistle
- the fact that Paul had nothing but praise for the church at Thessalonica and nothing to blame. They were the model church and the first one to which he wrote—but things would go downhill rapidly.

Why you should read 1 Thessalonians:
Ever wonder in this postmodern world if the Bible really is the Word of God, absolute in authority? You're not alone, and you're not the first. When Paul wrote to the Thessalonian Christians in the first century, the authority of the Bible was an issue. Paul commended them because they received the message as it is in truth, the Word of God, not the words of men. Let the Bible speak to you as the only book God ever wrote, the authoritative, eternal, accurate Word of God.

Second Thessalonians
The Book of the Day of the Lord

Written:
Author: Paul
Audience: the church at Thessalonica in northern Greece
Date: A.D. 51–52

Overview:
Subject: the apostle comforts the Thessalonian believers because of the persecution they endured and reassures them of Christ's coming to vindicate their cause
Setting: written from Corinth a few months after the first letter

Three keys:
Key chapter: 2 (the Day of the Lord)
Key verses: 1:7-10; 2:3-4, 7-12; 3:5
Key people: Paul, Silas, Timothy, the Thessalonian church

Book profile:
Number of chapters: 3
Number of verses: 47
Average reading time: 7 minutes

What to look for:
- Jesus Christ as the Coming Lord (1:7-8)
- the gentle and encouraging way Paul writes to his friends who need their mistaken beliefs corrected
- the strong and stern warning about what will happen to those who refuse to believe the truth of the gospel

Why you should read 2 Thessalonians:
When your friends reject the gospel and say something foolish like, "I don't mind going to hell; all my friends will be there," take your cue from Paul. His burden for the lost was real and it was significant, but he never allowed that burden to soften the truth of what awaited the lost if they continued to reject Jesus Christ as Savior. Let 2 Thessalonians increase your burden for unsaved friends and family. Never lose sight of what it means for those who risk spending eternity outside of God's presence.

First Timothy
The Book of Pastoral Counsel

Written:
Author: Paul
Audience: Timothy
Date: A.D. 63–66

Overview:
Subject: the teaching and behavior by which the church is to conduct itself
Setting: written from Macedonia, perhaps Philippi, after Paul's release from Roman imprisonment

Three keys:
Key chapters: 2 (the keys to an enduring ministry); 3 (the qualifications for church leaders)
Key verses: 1:17; 2:1-5; 3:1-13; 4:12, 14; 5:8, 17, 22; 6:6, 10-12
Key people: Paul, Timothy

Book profile:
Number of chapters: 6
Number of verses: 113
Average reading time: 14 minutes

What to look for:
- Jesus Christ as the Mediator Between God and Man (2:5)
- the emphasis of the apostle on sound doctrine that leads to godliness
- clues to the teaching and conduct that is becoming in the church

Why you should read 1 Timothy:
Hope is a precious commodity and getting rarer all the time. Alexander Pope said, "Hope springs eternal in the human breast," but for a lot of people, that spring is getting weaker. Let 1 Timothy restore hope to you. It is not found in what we do but in who we have. When Paul wrote to Timothy in his salutation, he referred to the "Lord Jesus Christ, our hope" (1:1). Hope is a noun. It's not primarily something you do; it's something you have when you have Jesus Christ as Savior. Read 1 Timothy and let your hope be strengthened.

Second Timothy
The Book of Final Ministry

Written:
Author: Paul
Audience: Timothy, Paul's own son in the faith
Date: A.D. 67

Overview:
Subject: the unchangeable authority and power of God's Holy Word
Setting: written during Paul's final imprisonment in Rome, just before his death

Three keys:
Key chapters: 2 (the metaphors of ministry); 3 (the certainty of God's Word in times of apostasy)
Key verses: 1:12, 16-18; 2:1-6, 15, 24; 3:1-7, 12, 14-16; 4:1-2, 6-8, 10, 13, 16-17
Key people: Paul, Timothy, Lois, Eunice, Luke, Mark, the household of Onesiphorus

Book profile:
Number of chapters: 4
Number of verses: 83
Average reading time: 8 minutes

What to look for:
- Jesus Christ as the One Who Stands With Us (4:17)
- the tone of finality in Paul's words as he writes the last letter of his apostleship
- the delightful metaphors for how we are to serve the Lord—as a son, a soldier, an athlete, a farmer, a workman

Why you should read 2 Timothy:
Let 2 Timothy remind you of a valuable lesson. When it appears that you are out on a limb for your faith, when you are standing all alone, remember that the Lord stands with you. He is there, providing strength and support even if others cannot see Him. Look for Him. He is there.

Titus
The Book of Church Order

Written:
Author: Paul
Audience: Titus, a young Greek being trained by Paul
Date: A.D. 63–66

Overview:
Subject: good works, sound doctrine, and church leadership on the island of Crete, where Titus ministered
Setting: written from Macedonia between Paul's imprisonments

Three keys:
Key chapters: 1 (the qualifications for church leaders); 2 (directions for sound doctrine and practice)
Key verses: 1:5-9; 2:3-5, 11-14; 3:4-7
Key people: Paul, Titus

Book profile:
Number of chapters: 3
Number of verses: 46
Average reading time: 6 minutes

What to look for:
- Jesus Christ as Our Great God and Savior (2:13)
- how Paul links the grace we enjoy in salvation with the godliness in living that should result
- evidences that the church on the island of Crete faced the same needs churches in Greece and Asia Minor did, such as qualified leadership, diligence in refuting false teachers, and avoiding contentious arguments

Why you should read Titus:
Tucked away in the shadow of Titus 2:13, a very powerful and prominent verse, is perhaps an even more important verse for you to remember. Titus 2:14 records the two reasons why Jesus died: (1) to redeem us from our sin, and (2) to purify us and make us a people marked out by godly lifestyles. Most Christians are aware of the first but not the second. Let the tiny epistle of Titus remind you how important it is that you are not only saved but set apart to God in purity.

Philemon
The Book of Brotherhood

Written:
Author: Paul
Audience: Philemon, a wealthy member of the Colossian church
Date: A.D. 60–62

Overview:
Subject: a runaway slave encounters Paul, trusts Christ, and returns to his Christian master
Setting: written from Rome while Paul was a prisoner

Three keys:
Key chapter: 1 (from slave to brother)
Key verses: 7, 10, 15-19, 20
Key people: Paul, Philemon, Onesimus

Book profile:
Number of chapters: 1
Number of verses: 25
Average reading time: 3 minutes

What to look for:
- Jesus Christ as the One Who Paid Our Debt (v. 18)
- the repeated subtleties Paul uses in gently pressuring Philemon to return the runaway slave Onesimus to the apostle
- Paul's usual method of letter writing: introduction, wish for grace and peace, thanksgiving and prayer, and then right to the issue at hand

Why you should read Philemon:
Faith in Christ is the great equalizer, so that even a runaway slave and his master are "brothers in the Lord." Onesimus had equal potential in serving the Lord as did his former master. Let this brief letter encourage you. It doesn't matter where you have come from; what matters is where you are going for Christ.

Hebrews
The Book of the Priesthood of Christ

Written:
Author: uncertain—perhaps Paul, Luke, Barnabas, Apollos, or Silas
Audience: Hebrew Christians who may have been considering a return to Judaism
Date: A.D. 68–70

Overview:
Subject: Christ offers the substance of the real thing after the Old Testament offered only glimpses of the real thing
Setting: written before the destruction of the temple in A.D. 70, but no one is certain from where

Three keys:
Key chapters: 1 (Jesus as Son, Creator, the Express Image of God); 4 (Jesus as Our Great High Priest); 7 (Jesus as Priest After Melchizedek); 9 (Jesus as Superior to Aaron); 11 (pilgrims on the walk of faith)
Key verses: 1:1-3; 2:3; 4:12-16; 5:5-6; 7:1-3, 11, 20-22, 24-27; 9:11-15, 20-22, 24-28; 10:4, 10, 31, 37; 11:1-3, 6; 12:1-2, 6, 11, 29; 13:5, 8, 20-21
Key people: Melchizedek, Aaron, Old Testament men and women of faith

Book profile:
Number of chapters: 13
Number of verses: 303
Average reading time: 40 minutes

What to look for:
- Jesus Christ as the Great High Priest (4:14)
- the frequent references to Jesus Christ as greater than the prophets, the angels, Moses, Aaron, the Old Testament priesthood, etc.
- the author's painstaking citations of Old Testament passages, more than eighty times in all, to convince his Jewish readers

Why you should read Hebrews:
Faith is not related to circumstances. Use this book to encourage your friends and yourself that when good things don't happen to you, it is not because you didn't have enough faith. In the great "Hall of Faith" chapter of Hebrews 11, the first half records the stories of those who had faith and were successful; the second half records the stories of those who had faith and were failures. Our faith rests in the righteous character of God, not in the things that happen to us.

James
The Book of Practical Christianity

Written:
Author: James, half brother of Jesus
Audience: first-century Jewish Christians living in Gentile communities in the Diaspora, those areas of the world outside of Judea where Jews lived
Date: A.D. 45–49

Overview:
Subject: genuine saving faith produces genuine Christian works
Setting: written from Jerusalem, prior to the Jerusalem Council held in A.D. 50

Three keys:
Key chapters: 1 (wisdom to face temptation); 2 (godly faith produces godly works); 3 (mind your tongue)
Key verses: 1:5-7, 17, 22; 2:10, 14, 17-18; 3:5-6, 8-10, 15, 17; 4:4, 6-8, 10, 17; 5:13-16, 20
Key people: James, Abraham, Job, Elijah, scattered Jewish believers

Book profile:
Number of chapters: 5
Number of verses: 108
Average reading time: 14 minutes

What to look for:
- Jesus Christ as the Lord Drawing Near (4:8)
- the authoritative way in which James instructs his readers; he issues fifty-four imperatives in five short chapters
- the many examples of both true religion and false profession

Why you should read James:
Have you heard about people who were so heavenly minded they were no earthly good? Apparently James had. Let his book encourage you to get some dirt under your fingernails. Let it persuade you to find someone for whom you can do practical acts of kindness. Let it orchestrate in your life the kind of religion that doesn't just talk. You will benefit greatly from James if your faith is tested, found true, and truly active.

First Peter
The Book of Grace Under Fire

Written:
Author: Peter
Audience: Jewish Christians scattered through Asia Minor
Date: A.D. 64–65

Overview:
Subject: the Christian will not be free from the difficulties of life but has hope in Christ through those difficulties
Setting: written from a Roman prison during the great persecutions under Nero

Three keys:
Key chapters: 1 (be holy in the midst of troubles); 2 (Jesus Christ, the Pattern for Suffering); 4 (how to handle persecution and suffering)
Key verses: 1:3-5, 7-12, 16, 23-25; 2:6-8, 21-25; 3:14-15, 17-18; 4:12-16; 5:6-8
Key people: Peter, Silvanus, Mark, believers throughout Asia Minor

Book profile:
Number of chapters: 5
Number of verses: 105
Average reading time: 15 minutes

What to look for:
- Jesus Christ as the Suffering Lamb (1:19)
- advice on how to bear up under all kinds of persecution
- evidences of hope in the midst of personal suffering

Why you should read 1 Peter:
How on earth can you be holy? How do you respond to persecution at the office or even around the house? When you try to live for Christ and get shot down, what do you do? The Letter of 1 Peter can help. Read it and learn how to remain holy in a world enamored with unholiness. Let it guide you in your responses to those who trouble you. And let it encourage you that God will not forget your appropriate responses to those who harass you.

Second Peter
The Book of the Last Days

Written:
Author: Peter
Audience: the church at large
Date: A.D. 66–67

Overview:
Subject: Christian diligence in light of the last days, the second coming of Christ, the judgment of the wicked, and the Day of the Lord
Setting: written perhaps from Rome to warn believers everywhere of false teachers and to exhort them to grow in the grace and knowledge of the Lord

Three keys:
Key chapters: 1 (how God transmitted His Holy Word); 2 (warning against apostate teachers)
Key verses: 1:19-21; 2:1-3, 13-17; 3:3-4, 9-10, 12-13, 18
Key people: Peter, Paul, those of like faith

Book profile:
Number of chapters: 3
Number of verses: 61
Average reading time: 8 minutes

What to look for:
- Jesus Christ as the Lord of Glory (1:16-17)
- encouragement to look forward to the Lord's return amid the encroaching darkness of the world
- evidences that Peter is more concerned about how his readers finish in their faith than how they first begin in it

Why you should read 2 Peter:
Dangers from within are always more threatening than dangers from without. Peter knew this, and his second epistle helps each of us be on guard against those within the church who question the basic doctrines of the faith, who twist the tried and true to come up with something untested and new, who advocate questionable practices that may lead to immorality. Let Peter's epistle guide you and help you guard what you know is true.

First John
The Book of Fellowship

Written:
Author: John
Audience: a pastoral letter sent to various congregations
Date: A.D. 85–95

Overview:
Subject: knowing you are at home in the family of God
Setting: written perhaps from Ephesus before John was banished to the island of Patmos

Three keys:
Key chapters: 1 (the relief of confession); 5 (the assurance of salvation)
Key verses: 1:3, 7, 9; 2:15; 3:1-3; 4:1-4, 10-12, 18-19; 5:11-13
Key person: John

Book profile:
Number of chapters: 5
Number of verses: 105
Average reading time: 13 minutes

What to look for:
- Jesus Christ as the Coming Son of God (2:28)
- although 1 John is often repetitious, look for slight variations in that repetition to reveal different nuances of meaning
- evidence that a believer can know for certain that he or she belongs to Christ

Why you should read 1 John:
This epistle is all about knowing and being sure. If you are troubled about your salvation, worried if it's real, wondering if something may happen between now and your last day on earth that will rob you of your place in heaven, let 1 John reassure you. It is a strong and reasoned defense of your ability to know you are saved. Read it with an open mind and an open heart, and you will walk away from it with assurance.

Second John
The Book of Love and Truth

Written:

Author: John

Audience: "the elect lady" (perhaps the proper female name Cyria, or Kuria, instead of the translation "the elect lady") and her household, perhaps the church that met in her house

Date: A.D. 85–95

Overview:

Subject: John warns against the corrupting influences of false teachers in the church, especially those who deny Christ's humanity

Setting: written perhaps from Ephesus before John was banished to the island of Patmos

Three keys:

Key chapter: 1 (love and truth)

Key verses: 4, 8, 10-11

Key people: the Elder (John), Cyria and her children

Book profile:

Number of chapters: 1

Number of verses: 13

Average reading time: 2 minutes

What to look for:

- Jesus Christ, the Son of God and Son of Man (v. 7)
- repeated warnings about aiding those who spread false doctrine
- evidence of John's belief that the truth is not "out there" but in Christ

Why you should read 2 John:

Do you believe that Mormons and Jehovah's Witnesses are nice people who just believe a little differently than other Christians? Well, they may be nice people, but their beliefs are not Christian. Let 2 John convince you that what you believe about Christ separates truth from error, Christianity from cultism. Those who do not believe Jesus Christ came in the flesh are against Christ. And those who know in a saving way both the Father and the Son believe that Jesus is God the Son just as much as they believe Jehovah is God the Father.

Third John
The Book of Warning Against Pride

Written:
Author: John
Audience: Gaius, a prominent Christian in a local church
Date: A.D. 85–95

Overview:
Subject: warning against pride and praise for hospitality
Setting: written perhaps from Ephesus before John was banished to the island of Patmos

Three keys:
Key chapter: 1 (be careful of those who love preeminence)
Key verses: 4, 9, 12
Key people: the Elder (John), Gaius, Diotrephes, Demetrius

Book profile:
Number of chapters: 1
Number of verses: 14
Average reading time: 2 minutes

What to look for:
- Jesus Christ as the Truth (vv. 3-4)
- the dramatic change of tone from joy to censure and back to joy in just fourteen verses
- the many ways we can spread the truth—by life, testimony, hospitality, unity, doing good, rebuking hypocrisy

Why you should read 3 John:
If you have children who are walking with the Lord, that's a great joy, isn't it? John felt that way about his "spiritual" children, those he had led to faith in Christ. The final epistle of John should encourage you to pray for your children, both those who are a part of your physical family and those who are a part of your extended spiritual family. Walking in truth is not only good for your children, but it's the ultimate personal hedge against falling prey to error.

Jude
The Book of Contending for the Faith

Written:
Author: Jude, half brother of Jesus Christ
Audience: Jewish Christians
Date: A.D. 67–68

Overview:
Subject: warning against false teachers and the judgment that awaits them
Setting: perhaps written from Jerusalem

Three keys:
Key chapter: 1 (contend for the faith)
Key verses: 3, 6, 24-25
Key people: Jude, James, Michael, Cain, Balaam, Korah

Book profile:
Number of chapters: 1
Number of verses: 25
Average reading time: 4 minutes

What to look for:
- Jesus Christ as the Coming Judge (vv. 14-15)
- Jude's concern that we wrestle with troublemakers while holding fast to the truth ourselves
- a breathtaking doxology concluding a tiny epistle concerned with apostasy

Why you should read Jude:
Jude mentions three Old Testament characters as bad role models, the kind of people we should avoid. Does that inspire you to make sure you are a positive role model to those watching you? Are you investing your life in others in a way that pleases God, benefits them, and enriches you? Let Jude persuade you to continue your positive influence in the lives of others, or convict you to begin that influence if it doesn't already exist.

Revelation
The Book of the Future

Written:
Author: John
Audience: the seven churches in Asia Minor, modern Turkey
Date: A.D. 95–96

Overview:
Subject: the curtain falls on this age with the activity of the Antichrist and rises again with Christ and eternity
Setting: written from the island of Patmos, in the eastern Mediterranean Sea, about events that would take place in the future

Three keys:
Key chapters: 1–3 (the seven churches); 4–5 (worship around the throne of God); 13 (the rise of the Antichrist); 19 (the coming of Christ in power and glory); 20 (the Millennium); 21 (the new heaven and new earth)
Key verses: 1:8, 19; 3:20; 4:8, 11; 5:1-5, 9, 12; 6:15-17; 7:11-14; 11:3, 7-12, 15; 13:1, 4, 11-12, 14-18; 16:16; 17:3-6; 19:11-16; 20:1-7, 10-15; 21:4, 6, 16; 22:1-5, 7, 12-13, 16-20
Key people: John, the twenty-four elders, the Lion of the Tribe of Judah, the Antichrist, the Beast, the False Prophet, the Two Witnesses, the 144,000

Book profile:
Number of chapters: 22
Number of verses: 404
Average reading time: 1 hour, 6 minutes

What to look for:
- Jesus Christ as the Lord's Christ (11:15)
- a story of future events that is not chronological in order but rather thematic in treatment
- a blessing just for reading this book (1:3), even if you don't understand everything

Why you should read Revelation:
Revelation is a reminder that we are not fatalists, tripping headlong toward an indeterminate end. We are moving toward a culmination, and that culmination may be a lot nearer than anyone realizes. Use Revelation as a reminder that no one knows the day nor the hour when the Son of Man will come again (Matt. 25:13). Be caught up in your reading of God's Word, and be ready to be caught up with God's Son. Maranatha!

Meet the Authors

Agur. The author, or perhaps compiler or collector, of the words of wisdom recorded in Proverbs 30. He was the son of Jakeh (Prov. 30:1). His prophecy was not so much a prediction of the future as it was a series of wise sayings or weighty maxims (Heb. massá). Little else is known of him.

Amos. One of the most colorful characters in the Old Testament, yet with humble beginnings. He was a simple sheepherder who once recalled, "I was no prophet, nor was I a son of a prophet, but I was a herdsman and a tender of sycamore fruit" (Amos 7:14). He prophesied in Israel during a period of almost unprecedented prosperity but equally unprecedented social and religious corruption (Amos 2:6-8; 5:11-12).

Apollos. A Jewish man from Alexandria, Egypt, who had come to faith in Christ Jesus. The university in Alexandria was world-renowned for its school of rhetoric, and Apollos was one of its star pupils. He was a man mighty in the Scriptures, but he knew only of the baptism of John. Priscilla and Aquila, a Jewish couple who also had trusted Christ as Messiah and were living in Ephesus, took Apollos aside and instructed him in the deeper things of the Word of God (Acts 18:26). Apollos was an eloquent spokesman for God in the first century and possibly the author of Hebrews.

Asaph. One of the premier musicians of the Bible, Asaph was a Levite of the Gershonite family. He was the praise and worship leader of Israel in David's and Solomon's time (1 Chron. 16:37). He led the singing, played the cymbals, and instructed others in the music of Jehovah (Neh. 7:44). Twelve psalms are credited to Asaph, a man of deep spiritual and contemplative spirit.

Barnabas. His first name was Joseph, and Barnabas was his surname (the King James Version calls it a surname, while the modern English versions indicate it was his nickname—see Acts 4:36). He was a Levite from Cyprus who first became a financial supporter of those who needed assistance in the Jerusalem church (Acts 4:36ff). Then he was used of God as a recruiter to get Saul of Tarsus to come as a teacher in the Antioch church (Acts 11:22-26). Finally, he became a full-fledged missionary himself as he joined Saul, now Paul the apostle, on the first missionary journey. Barnabas represents the full cycle of service for Jesus. He is included here as a possible author of the Book of Hebrews.

Daniel. A young teen of the royal Jewish family who was carried into Babylonian captivity by King Nebuchadnezzar (Dan. 1). God gifted Daniel with understanding in visions and dreams, and using this gift, Daniel was able to interpret one of the great prophecies of all time— the prophecy of the four kingdoms represented in the great image of King Nebuchadnezzar (Dan. 2). Best remembered for his face-off against the lions in their den, everything about Daniel's life pointed to the sovereignty and wisdom of God.

David. The simple shepherd boy who became Israel's greatest king, David was a giant killer (Goliath), a city planner (Jerusalem), and a musical composer (his psalms). He was a man after God's own heart (1 Sam. 13:14; Acts 13:22). But more than anything else, David was the head of a dynasty, a family that would bring into the world the Son of God (Matt. 1:1-21), the Messiah of Israel (Matt. 1:1, 16; 16:16), the Savior of the world (Luke 2:11; John 1:29)—Jesus Christ.

Elihu. The youngest and final of Job's friends who came to commiserate with him but ended up becoming his nemesis. Elihu spoke like some young seminary student, filled with a theoretical knowledge of theology but inexperienced in practical intimacy with God. When Eliphas, Bildad, and Zophar ended their inquisition of Job, Elihu began his. We know nothing of him except that he was the son of Barachel the Buzite (Job 32:2-6). That would make him an Aramean or what today we would call a Syrian. He is suggested as a possible author of the Book of Job.

Ethan. An Old Testament man of remarkable skill and wisdom. The superscription over Psalm 89 notes that it is a maschil, or poem of contemplation, composed by Ethan the Ezrahite, indicating his literary skill. His wisdom is seen in comparison with that of Solomon, who was said to be "wiser than all men—than Ethan the Ezrahite, and Heman, Chalcol, and Darda" (1 Kings 4:31). That's pretty good company.

Ezekiel. A member of a priestly family (Ezek. 1:3) and a Hebrew prophet of the Exile when the Jews were living as captives in Babylon. Ezekiel was both a powerful preacher and a powerful writer, using allegory, word pictures, and symbolic actions to enhance the impression of his message. God called him "son of man" eighty-seven times in his writing, apparently to remind the prophet that he was just a man and was totally dependent on God for his message.

Ezra. A famous Jewish priest (direct descendant of Aaron, Moses' brother and high priest of Israel) and scribe, and a friend and coworker of Nehemiah. He is the main character of the book that bears his name and a key figure in the Book of Nehemiah. Ezra was a great reformer among the Jews who returned to Jerusalem from Babylonian captivity. He was the man who read from the Bible and explained its meaning to the people while they drank it all in from morning until midday (Neh. 8).

Habakkuk. Very little is known about this man, one of the strangest prophets of the Old Testament. He gives us no information about himself in his prophecy. What we do know is that Habakkuk's writing is, by and large, a complaint against God—that God allowed His own nation to be destroyed for its wickedness by a nation even more wicked. Habakkuk didn't understand. He was either a man living very close to God or one who liked to live dangerously.

Haggai. A man who lived soon after the Babylonian captivity and was a contemporary with the prophet Zechariah (Hag. 1:1; Zech. 1:1). Haggai was the conscience of the Jews who returned to Jerusalem, reestablished daily worship, and began building the temple. When they soon became complacent about working for God and became content to dwell in their semi-luxurious houses, Haggai wrote to shame them, wake them up, and get them back to work. God used him to change their attitude from discouragement to victory.

Heman. Like Ethan the Ezrahite, Heman was both a skilled and wise man. Psalm 88 is attributed to him. Some people think that Ezrahite means "Zerahite," and if that is the case, this Heman may be the grandson of Judah through Zerah (1 Chron. 2:6). Beyond that, we know nothing of him.

Hosea. Of all the Old Testament prophetic writings, Hosea's is the only one that comes from Israel's northern kingdom. Hosea lived during a time of great economic prosperity but also great unfaithfulness toward Jehovah. God asked the prophet to marry a woman whom the Lord knew would be unfaithful to him. This was done to graphically depict Israel's unfaithfulness to God. It takes a man who has a profound trust in the wisdom and sovereignty of God to do that.

Isaiah. Perhaps the major prophet of the Bible. Isaiah's father, Amoz, may have been a person of some prominence, because Isaiah is called "the son of Amoz" thirteen times in the book. He was married and had two children, to whom he gave significant but almost unpronounceable names—Shear-Jashub (Isa. 7:3) and Maher-Shalal-Hash-Baz (Isa. 8:3). Isaiah was the great Old Testament herald of the coming Messiah. His book, which contains sixty-six chapters (just the Bible contains sixty-six books), has been called the Bible in miniature because it tells the story of God's love and redemption.

James. Four prominent men bear the name James in the New Testament. The best known is James the brother of John and disciple of the Lord (Matt. 4:21). Then there is James the son of Alphaeus, another of Jesus' disciples (Matt. 10:3), and James the father of one of Jesus' disciples (Luke 6:16). But the one who authored the epistle that bears his name is the James who served as one of the pillars in the church at Jerusalem (Acts 21:18). That James is the half brother of the Lord Jesus (Matt. 13:55).

Jeremiah. Sometimes referred to as Jeremy or Jeremias (Matt. 2:17; 16:14), Jeremiah is one of the greatest of the Hebrew prophets, along with Isaiah. He was a Jerusalem suburbanite, having been born in Anathoth, just a couple of miles northeast of Jerusalem in the seventh century B.C. Jeremiah is often called "the weeping prophet" for the sorrowful lamentation he made over the destruction of his beloved Jerusalem. Late in his life Jeremiah was forced to flee to Egypt, where tradition says he was placed in a hollow log and sawn in two by his rebellious countrymen. He died an old man.

Job. Because Job the person stands outside of the Abrahamic Covenant, the family of Israel, and is a freestanding figure in Old Testament history, it is difficult to say much about him with certainty. He lived in the land of Uz, sometimes identified with Bashan, the highlands east of the Sea of Galilee, and sometimes with the country southeast of the Promised Land in the desert of Arabia. What we know for sure about Job is that he revered God and shunned evil. He was "the greatest of all the people of the East" (Job 1:3).

Joel. His name means "The Lord [Yahweh] is God," and he is the son of Pethuel. Beyond that, Joel's life and times are a mystery to us. Joel does not date his writing in any way. His name was a common one in Old Testament Israel, for thirteen other men mentioned in the Bible also bear this name. What is unique to Joel, however, is the event that precipitated his writing. It was a devastating plague of locusts that the prophet used as an occasion to call the Jews to repentance.

John. The author who wrote the Gospel of John, the three epistles of John, and the Revelation that concludes the New Testament is not John the Baptist, who was beheaded for his strong and personal preaching against sin (Mark 6). This John was the fisherman turned apostle and disciple, who was the brother of James and the son of Zebedee (Matt. 4:21). He died an old man in Ephesus, after being banished for many years to the island of Patmos (Rev. 1:9). There he received the Revelation, the greatest apocalyptic look into the future in all literature.

Jonah. We know more about Jonah than most prophets of the Old Testament. He was a prophet of Israel, the son of Amittai (Jonah 1:1), and he lived in the town of Gath Hepher in the tribe of Zebulun (2 Kings 14:25). That means Jonah was a prophet from Galilee. Guess the Pharisees were wrong when they said that no prophet had ever come from Galilee (John 7:52)!

Joshua. Born in Egyptian slavery and given the name Hoshea (Oshea), meaning "salvation" (Num. 13:8; Deut. 32:44), by his father, Nun. Joshua became Moses' lieutenant during the Exodus and defeated the Amalekites when they viciously attacked Israel (Ex. 17:9). Upon Moses' death he became the captain of Israel, leading the people across the Jordan River and to victory at the Battle of Jericho. Of Joshua it was said that he "wholly followed the Lord" (Num. 32:12).

Jude. Half a dozen men in the New Testament bore this name, a derivative of Judah or Judas, but only one was the half brother of the Lord Jesus (Matt. 13:55). While he did not express saving faith in Jesus during our Lord's life, Jude became an ardent follower after His Resurrection (Acts 1:14). It is interesting that neither Jude nor James mentions his family relationship to the Lord in his epistle, but both freely admit they were servants of Jesus (James 1:1; Jude 1).

Korah's Sons. The ancestor of these men was not the infamous Korah who resisted Moses' authority and consequently was consumed when the ground opened up and swallowed him (Num. 16). This Korah was a Levite whose descendants were doorkeepers and musicians at the tabernacle and later at the temple (Ex. 6:24; 1 Chron. 6:22). The musician sons of Korah are said to have written Psalms 42, 44–49, 84–85, and 87–88.

Lemuel, King. The name Lemuel means "devoted to God" and is found only twice in the Bible (Prov. 31:1, 4). This king is unknown apart from these references but is said to have been taught the maxims in Proverbs 31:2-9 by his mother. Likely this is a name by which Solomon refers to himself, because he best fits the wisdom represented in this chapter.

Luke. A man of education and culture, a follower of Jesus Christ, and the author of the third Gospel, Luke was a physician by profession (Col. 4:14). He was also a coworker with the apostle Paul (Philem. 24), accompanying him on many of his journeys (2 Tim. 4:11), perhaps as personal physician. In addition to his Gospel, Luke wrote the historical account of the early church we know as the Acts of the Apostles, or simply Acts, sometimes writing in the first person (Acts 16:10-17).

Malachi. The name of the author of the last book of the Old Testament means "my messenger" and is so translated in Malachi 3:1, an obvious play on words. Beyond this, nothing is known of the prophet except that he was one of the last during the Old Testament period, later even than Haggai and Zechariah. He prophesied to God's people, who had become lax with regard to worship and respect for God and His Word.

Mark. Mentioned by name ten times in the New Testament, John was his Jewish name and Mark or Marcus his Roman name. His home became a safe house for the early Jerusalem Christians (Acts 12:12). He accompanied Paul and Barnabas on their first missionary journey (Acts 12:25) but was the flashpoint of disagreement on the second (Acts 15:37-38). So Barnabas took Mark and went to Cyprus; Paul took Silas and went to Asia Minor and eventually Greece. Later Mark again worked with Paul (Philem. 24) and eventually with Peter (1 Pet. 5:13).

Matthew. The son of Alphaeus (Mark 2:14), Matthew was a Jew working as a tax collector for the hated Romans. His Jewish name was Levi (Mark 2:14; Luke 5:27); he likely changed it to Matthew, meaning "gift of Yahweh," when he became one of Jesus' disciples. Although he is well known to us today because of his Gospel, apart from the lists of disciples' names (Matt. 10:3; Mark 3:18; Acts 1:13), Matthew is nowhere else mentioned by name in the New Testament.

Micah. Seven men in the Old Testament were given this name, which is the short form of Micaiah (or Michael), meaning "Who is like Jehovah?" (Mic. 1:1; Jer. 26:18). Micah was a man from Moresheth Gath (Mic. 1:14), which likely was a town on the border between Judah and the Philistine territory, about thirty miles southwest of Jerusalem. He was a contemporary of Isaiah and Hosea.

Mordecai. The hero of the Book of Esther, Mordecai was a Benjamite who had been deported during the reign of King Jeconiah or, more likely, Jehoiachin of Judah (Esther 2:5-6). He lived in Shushan (Susa), the Persian capital, and was the guardian of his cousin, Esther, whose parents were dead (Esther 2:7). Mordecai discovered a plot at the palace to kill the king (Esther 2:21-23) and foiled that plot. Later he was used by God to arrange for Esther to save the Jewish people from annihilation (Esther 8). He is suggested as the author of the Book of Esther.

Moses. The national hero of Israel who delivered God's chosen people from Egyptian bondage, Moses spent forty years being raised in the household of Pharaoh, thinking he was somebody (Ex. 2:1-10). Then he spent forty years on the backside of the desert finding out he was a nobody (Ex. 2:11-3:1). Finally, he spent forty years leading the people of God from their 430-year-long national nightmare, finding out what God can do with a "nobody." Moses is an example of a meek and humble person who rises to the occasion in the strength of the Lord.

Nahum. The shortened form of the name Nehemiah, Nahum is called an Elkoshite, or a resident of the village of Elkosh. While the church father Jerome says that he visited a town in Galilee known as Elkosh, others have speculated that it was a village in southern Judah. In fact, no one knows for sure where it was. The Book of Nahum is a poem, a literary masterpiece, predicting the fall of Nineveh, the capital of the Assyrian empire.

Nehemiah. The son of Hachaliah, Nehemiah was the cupbearer to King Artaxerxes of Persia (Neh. 1:11). When he learned the sad state of Jerusalem, he requested that the king send him back to his native city to rebuild it. Artaxerxes made Nehemiah governor of the Persian province of Judah, and Nehemiah energized the Jews of Jerusalem to rebuild the city wall. Nehemiah was a born leader, a man of courage, vision, and action.

Obadiah. No less than thirteen men in the Old Testament bear this name, but none so well (the name means "servant of Jehovah") as the prophet who wrote the prophecy against Edom. We could write all we know of this man on the back of a postage stamp—and have room left over. The Book of Obadiah is not dated, but it is timeless because it deals with anti-Semites, those who hate the people God loves.

Paul. A Jew born at Tarsus in Cilicia (south-central Turkey, just inland from the northeast corner of the Mediterranean Sea), Saul was a Roman citizen (Acts 22:28) because Tarsus was a Roman colony. He used his Jewish name, Saul, until sometime after his conversion on the road to Damascus (Acts 13:9). There he met Jesus Christ in a saving way, and the persecutor became the preacher. Paul was a Jewish rabbi, called to be the Apostle to the Gentiles, and as such became the bridge between the Jewish and Gentile factions of the early church. God used him to record much of Christian doctrine as we know it today.

Peter. The most prominent of the twelve disciples (always mentioned first in the lists of disciples), Peter was called to discipleship—along with his brother, Andrew, and fishing partners James and John—and never looked back (Mark 1:14-20). He was a native of Bethsaida (John 1:44), and his original name was Simon, a Greek name, or Symeon, a popular Hebrew name (Acts 15:14). Jesus gave him the name Cephas (John 1:42), meaning "rock" or "stone." Unschooled in rabbinical law (Acts 4:13), Peter nevertheless became the spokesman for the twelve and the principal preacher of Christianity among the Jews after the resurrection of Christ.

Samuel. Often called the last of the judges (1 Sam. 7:6, 15-17) and the first of the prophets (1 Sam. 3:20; Acts 3:24; 13:20), Samuel was the son of a devout couple, Elkanah and Hannah of Ramathaim Zophim in the hill country of Ephraim. Presented to God for service as a small child, Samuel was raised in Shiloh by Eli the priest. There he grew and eventually made his home in Ramah, where he administered justice as a judge and priest and anointed first Saul (1 Sam. 10:1) and then David (1 Sam. 16:13) as king over Israel.

Silas. A name found only in the Book of Acts, Silas was a Roman citizen (Acts 16:37) sent with Paul and Barnabas by the Jerusalem church to deliver a letter to the church at Antioch (Acts 15:22-23). When Paul determined not to take John Mark on his second missionary journey, Silas was chosen to accompany him. He shared a cell in the Philippian jail with Paul (Acts 16:23-24) and remained the apostle's coworker and envoy. He joins Paul in the salutation of 1 and 2 Thessalonians using the name Silvanus.

Solomon. The second son of David by Bathsheba, Solomon was chosen to succeed his father on Israel's throne (1 Kings 1:37-39). He was a man of great wisdom (1 Kings 3:16-28) and great wealth (1 Kings 10:1-23), both of which were gifts from God (Eccl. 5:18-19). Solomon was a sensitive soul, the author of 3,000 proverbs and composer of 1,005 songs. Yet he took many foreign wives (1 Kings 11:1), which weakened Israel's resolve to worship only the Lord. As a result the kingdom was divided after Solomon's death (1 Kings 12:16) into the ten tribes to the north, called Israel, and the two tribes to the south, called Judah.

Zechariah. A very popular name among Jewish families (twenty-eight men bear this name in the Old Testament), Zechariah the prophet came from a long line of priests, being the son of Berechiah and grandson of Iddo (Zech. 1:1). This means Zechariah held the dual office of prophet and priest (Zech. 1:7). He returned from Babylonian captivity with Zerubbabel. Still, twenty years after their return, the temple lay in ruins. God raised up Haggai and Zechariah to encourage the Jews to get busy and rebuild the temple, and they did.

Zephaniah. Likely related to the kings of Judah and thus part of the royal court family (see his pedigree in Zeph. 1:1), Zephaniah was a contemporary of Nahum and Habakkuk. Although he was raised among royalty, he was nevertheless fearless in his denunciation of the evils of the day (1:12-18; 3:1-7). Zephaniah was the last of Israel's prophets to prophesy before the Babylonian captivity.

Appendix B

Books, Chapters, and Verses of the Bible

OLD TESTAMENT

Book	Chapters	Verses
Genesis	50	1,533
Exodus	40	1,213
Leviticus	27	859
Numbers	36	1,288
Deuteronomy	34	959
Joshua	24	658
Judges	21	618
Ruth	4	85
1 Samuel	31	810
2 Samuel	24	695
1 Kings	22	816
2 Kings	25	719
1 Chronicles	29	942
2 Chronicles	36	822
Ezra	10	280
Nehemiah	13	406
Esther	10	167
Job	42	1,070
Psalms	150	2,461

NEW TESTAMENT

Acts 28 1,007

Romans 16 433

1 Corinthians.....................16 437

2 Corinthians.....................13 257

Galatians 6 149

Ephesians.............................6 155

Philippians 4 104

Colossians............................4...................................95

1 Thessalonians ....5....................................89

2 Thessalonians ....3....................................47

1 Timothy.............................6 113

2 Timothy ....4...................................83

Titus.....................................3...................................46

Philemon..............................1...................................25

Hebrews 13 303

James 5 108

1 Peter 5 105

2 Peter ....3...................................61

1 John...................................5 105

2 John...................................1...................................13

3 John...................................1...................................14

Jude ....1...................................25

Revelation 22 404

Appendix C

Average Reading Time

Mark ....1 1/2 hours
Daniel ....1 1/4 hours
Revelation ....1 1/4 hours
1 Kings...1 1/4 hours
Romans..1 hour
Nehemiah ....1 hour
1 Corinthians..1 hour
2 Corinthians ....3/4 hour
Ezra..3/4 hour
Hebrews..3/4 hour
Esther...1/2 hour
Ecclesiastes..1/2 hour
Galatians...1/2 hour
Hosea...1/2 hour
Amos ....1/2 hour
Ephesians...1/2 hour
Zechariah...1/2 hour
Lamentations..1/4 hour
Ruth ....1/4 hour
Philippians...1/4 hour
Song of Solomon...1/4 hour
Colossians..1/4 hour
Joel..1/4 hour
1 Thessalonians ....1/4 hour
2 Thessalonians ....1/4 hour
Obadiah...1/4 hour
1 Timothy ....1/4 hour
2 Timothy ....1/4 hour
Jonah ....1/4 hour

Titus ....1/4 hour
Philemon ....1/4 hour
Micah ....1/4 hour
James ....1/4 hour
Nahum ....1/4 hour
1 Peter..1/4 hour
2 Peter..1/4 hour
Habakkuk..1/4 hour
Zephaniah ....1/4 hour
1 John...1/4 hour
2 John...1/4 hour
3 John...1/4 hour
Haggai ....1/4 hour
Jude..1/4 hour
Malachi...1/4 hour

Appendix D

Five-Star
One-Year Sunday Reading Plan

A plan to read your Bible one book at a time by reading Sundays only. If you prefer to read on Saturdays only (or any other day of the week), you could do that instead. By following this five-star plan you will complete your reading in one year of Sundays. Be sure to record the date on which you read each book.

1st Month	Book	Time Required	Date Read
1st Sunday	Genesis	3 1/4 hours	_____
2nd Sunday	Romans	1 hour	_____
3rd Sunday	Exodus	2 1/2 hours	_____
4th Sunday	1 Samuel	2 1/2 hours	_____

2nd Month	Book	Time Required	Date Read
1st Sunday	2 Samuel	1 3/4 hours	_____
2nd Sunday	Phill.; Col.	1/4 hour each	_____
3rd Sunday	Leviticus	2 hours	_____
4th Sunday	Numbers	3 hours	_____

3rd Month	Book	Time Required	Date Read
1st Sunday	Deuteronomy	2 1/4 hours	_____
2nd Sunday	1, 2 Peter; Jude	1/4 hour each	_____

			Date Read
3rd Sunday	Joshua	1 3/4 hours	_____
4th Sunday	Philemon; James	1/4 hour each	_____

4th Month	**Book**	**Time Required**	**Date Read**
1st Sunday	Judges	1 3/4 hours	_____
2nd Sunday	Song; Ruth; Malachi	1/4 hour each	_____
3rd Sunday	Matthew	2 1/4 hours	_____
4th Sunday	1, 2 Tim.; Titus	1/4 hour each	_____

5th Month	**Book**	**Time Required**	**Date Read**
1st Sunday	Isaiah	3 1/2 hours	_____
2nd Sunday	Acts	2 1/2 hours	_____
3rd Sunday	1 Chronicles	2 hours	_____
4th Sunday	2 Chronicles	2 1/2 hours	_____

6th Month	**Book**	**Time Required**	**Date Read**
1st Sunday	Joel; Obad.; Hab.	1/4 hour each	_____
2nd Sunday	1 Cor.	1 hour	_____
3rd Sunday	2 Cor.	3/4 hour	_____
4th Sunday	Psalms	3 3/4 hours	_____

7th Month	**Book**	**Time Required**	**Date Read**
1st Sunday	Jeremiah	3 3/4 hours	_____
2nd Sunday	Zeph.; Hag.; Zech.	1 hour	_____

3rd Sunday	Mark	1 1/2 hours	_____
4th Sunday	Ephesians	1/2 hour	_____

8th Month	**Book**	**Time Required**	**Date Read**
1st Sunday	1 Kings	1 1/4 hours	_____
2nd Sunday	2 Kings	2 hours	_____
3rd Sunday	Amos	1/2 hour	_____
4th Sunday	Hosea	1/2 hour	_____

9th Month	**Book**	**Time Required**	**Date Read**
1st Sunday	Luke	2 1/4 hours	_____
2nd Sunday	Galatians	1/2 hour	_____
3rd Sunday	Ezekiel	3 1/4 hours	_____
4th Sunday	Lamentations	1/4 hour	_____

10th Month	**Book**	**Time Required**	**Date Read**
1st Sunday	Job	2 hours	_____
2nd Sunday	Ecclesiastes	1/2 hour	_____
3rd Sunday	John	2 hours	_____
4th Sunday	Esther	1/2 hour	_____

11th Month	**Book**	**Time Required**	**Date Read**
1st Sunday	Ezra; Neh.	1 3/4 hours	_____
2nd Sunday	Hebrews	3/4 hour	_____
3rd Sunday	Proverbs	1 1/2 hours	_____
4th Sunday	1 & 2 Thess.	1/4 hour each	_____

12th Month	**Book**	**Time Required**	**Date Read**
1st Sunday	Daniel	1 1/4 hours	_____

2nd Sunday	1, 2, 3 John	1/4 hour each	_____
3rd Sunday	Jonah; Micah; Nahum	1/4 hour each	_____
4th Sunday	Revelation	1 1/4 hours	_____

Appendix E

Five-Star
Six-Month Reading Plan

A plan to read your Bible one book at a time by reading just two days a week and one weekend day. You will complete your reading in six months with this five-star plan. Be sure to record the date on which you read each book.

1st Month	Book	Time Required	Date Read
1st Monday	Ruth	1/4 hour	_____
1st Friday	Zechariah	1/2 hour	_____
1st Sunday	Psalms	3 3/4 hours	_____
2nd Tuesday	Philippians	1/4 hour	_____
2nd Saturday	1 Kings	1 1/4 hours	_____
3rd Monday	Song of Solomon	1/4 hour	_____
3rd Friday	Romans	1 hour	_____
3rd Sunday	Revelation	1 1/4 hours	_____
4th Tuesday	Colossians	1/4 hour	_____
4th Thursday	Ephesians	1/2 hour	_____
4th Saturday	Jeremiah	3 3/4 hours	_____

2nd Month	Book	Time Required	Date Read
1st Monday	Joel	1/4 hour	_____
1st Friday	Amos	1/2 hour	_____
1st Sunday	Leviticus	2 hours	_____

2nd Tuesday	1 Thessalonians	1/4 hour	11/3/12
2nd Thursday	2 Thessalonians	1/4 hour	11/15/12
2nd Saturday	Daniel	1 1/4 hours	1/20/13
3rd Monday	Nehemiah	1 hour	3/7/13
3rd Friday	Mark	1 1/2 hours	_____
3rd Sunday	Isaiah	3 1/2 hours	_____
4th Tuesday	Obadiah	1/4 hour	_____
4th Saturday	Proverbs	1 1/2 hours	_____

3rd Month	**Book**	**Time Required**	**Date Read**
1st Monday	1 Timothy	1/4 hour	_____
1st Friday	Hosea	1/2 hour	_____
1st Sunday	Ezekiel	3 1/4 hours	_____
2nd Tuesday	2 Timothy	1/4 hour	_____
2nd Thursday	Jonah	1/4 hour	_____
2nd Saturday	Judges	1 3/4 hours	_____
3rd Monday	Titus	1/4 hour	_____
3rd Friday	Galatians	1/2 hour	_____
3rd Sunday	Joshua	1 3/4 hours	_____
4th Tuesday	Philemon	1/4 hour	_____
4th Saturday	Genesis	3 1/4 hours	_____

4th Month	**Book**	**Time Required**	**Date Read**
1st Monday	Micah	1/4 hour	_____
1st Friday	1 Corinthians	1 hour	_____
1st Sunday	2 Samuel	1 3/4 hours	_____
2nd Tuesday	James	1/4 hour	_____
2nd Saturday	Numbers	3 hours	_____
3rd Monday	Nahum	1/4 hour	_____

3rd Friday	Lamentations	1/4 hour	_____
3rd Sunday	Job	2 hours	_____
4th Tuesday	1 Peter	1/4 hour	_____
4th Thursday	2 Peter	1/4 hour	_____
4th Saturday	1 Chronicles	2 hours	_____

5th Month	**Book**	**Time Required**	**Date Read**
1st Monday	Habakkuk	1/4 hour	_____
1st Friday	Zephaniah	1/4 hour	_____
1st Sunday	Exodus	2 1/2 hours	_____
2nd Tuesday	1 John	1/4 hour	_____
2nd Thursday	2 Kings	2 hours	_____
2nd Saturday	Luke	2 1/4 hours	_____
3rd Monday	2 John	1/4 hour	_____
3rd Friday	3 John	1/4 hour	_____
3rd Sunday	Acts	2 1/2 hours	_____
4th Tuesday	Haggai	1/4 hour	_____
4th Saturday	John	2 hours	_____

6th Month	**Book**	**Time Required**	**Date Read**
1st Monday	Jude	1/4 hour	_____
1st Friday	Esther	1/2 hour	_____
1st Sunday	1 Samuel	2 1/2 hours	_____
2nd Tuesday	2 Corinthians	3/4 hour	_____
2nd Thursday	Ecclesiastes	1/2 hour	_____
2nd Saturday	2 Chronicles	2 1/2 hours	_____
3rd Monday	Malachi	1/4 hour	_____
3rd Friday	Ezra	3/4 hour	_____
3rd Sunday	Matthew	2 1/4 hours	_____

| 4th Tuesday | Hebrews | 3/4 hour | _____ |
| 4th Saturday | Deuteronomy | 2 1/4 hours | _____ |

Five-Star
Three-Month Reading Plan

If you're looking for a real challenge and want to read the Bible as expediently as possible in order to understand the complete message of the Book, this reading plan is for you. Be sure to record the date on which you read the books.

1st Month	Book	Time Required	Date Read
1st Monday	Ruth; Philippians	1/4 hour each	_____
1st Wednesday	Zechariah	1/2 hour	_____
1st Friday	Song; Colossians	1/4 hour each	_____
1st Saturday	1 Kings	1 1/4 hours	_____
1st Sunday	Psalms	3 3/4 hours	_____
2nd Tuesday	Joel; 1 Thess.	1/4 hour each	_____
2nd Thursday	Hosea	1/2 hour	_____
2nd Saturday	Genesis	3 1/4 hours	_____
2nd Sunday	Proverbs	1 1/2 hours	_____
3rd Monday	2 Thess.; Obadiah	1/4 hour each	_____
3rd Wednesday	Ephesians	1/2 hour	_____
3rd Friday	1, 2 Timothy	1/4 hour each	_____
3rd Saturday	Exodus	2 1/2 hours	_____
3rd Sunday	Acts	2 1/2 hours	_____
4th Tuesday	Jonah; Titus	1/4 hour each	_____
4th Thursday	Galatians	1/2 hour	_____

4th Saturday	Numbers	3 hours	_____
4th Sunday	Mark	1 1/2 hours	_____

2nd Month	Book	Time Required	Date Read
1st Monday	Lamentations	1/4 hour	_____
1st Wednesday	Ezra	3/4 hour	_____
1st Friday	Philemon; Micah	1/4 hour each	_____
1st Saturday	1 Samuel	2 1/2 hours	_____
1st Sunday	Matthew	2 1/4 hours	_____
2nd Tuesday	Ecclesiastes	1/2 hour	_____
2nd Thursday	James; Nahum	1/4 hour each	_____
2nd Saturday	Luke	2 1/4 hours	_____
2nd Sunday	Leviticus	2 hours	_____
3rd Monday	1, 2 Peter	1/4 hour each	_____
3rd Wednesday	Daniel	1 1/4 hours	_____
3rd Friday	Esther	1/2 hour	_____
3rd Saturday	Isaiah	3 1/2 hours	_____
3rd Sunday	Judges	1 3/4 hours	_____
4th Tuesday	Habakkuk	1/4 hour	_____
4th Thursday	1, 2, 3 John	1/4 hour each	_____
4th Saturday	Joshua	1 3/4 hours	_____
4th Sunday	Ezekiel	3 1/4 hours	_____

3rd Month	Book	Time Required	Date Read
1st Monday	Amos	1/2 hour	_____
1st Wednesday	1 Corinthians	1 hour	_____
1st Friday	2 Corinthians	3/4 hour	_____
1st Saturday	Jeremiah	3 3/4 hours	_____
1st Sunday	2 Samuel	1 3/4 hours	_____

2nd Tuesday	Zephaniah	1/4 hour	_____
2nd Thursday	Romans	1 hour	_____
2nd Saturday	1 Chronicles	2 hours	_____
2nd Sunday	2 Chronicles	2 1/2 hours	_____
3rd Monday	Haggai; Jude	1/4 hour each	_____
3rd Wednesday	Nehemiah	1 hour	_____
3rd Friday	Job	2 hours	_____
3rd Saturday	Deuteronomy	2 1/4 hours	_____
3rd Sunday	2 Kings	2 hours	_____
4th Tuesday	Malachi	1/4 hour	_____
4th Thursday	Hebrews	3/4 hour	_____
4th Saturday	John	2 hours	_____
4th Sunday	Revelation	1 1/4 hours	_____

Four-Star
Weekend Reading Plan

Read in thirty-minute blocks of time over adjacent weekends to read your Bible one book at a time. For those who cannot read for more than half an hour at a time, or cannot read a book all the way through in one sitting, this is the next-best plan to maintain continuity and context. Plus, it allows you to read the Bible in order and only involves weekends. Start any weekend you like. Be sure to record the date on which you read each book.

OLD TESTAMENT

1st Weekend   **Date Read**

Genesis	1/2 hour	_____
Genesis	1/2 hour	_____
Genesis	1/2 hour	_____

2nd Weekend   **Date Read**

Genesis	1/2 hour	_____
Genesis	1/2 hour	_____
Genesis	1/2 hour	_____
Genesis	1/2 hour	_____

3rd Weekend		Date Read
Exodus	1/2 hour	_____
Exodus	1/2 hour	_____
Exodus	1/2 hour	_____
Exodus	1/2 hour	_____
Exodus	1/2 hour	_____

4th Weekend		Date Read
Leviticus	1/2 hour	_____
Leviticus	1/2 hour	_____
Leviticus	1/2 hour	_____
Leviticus	1/2 hour	_____

5th Weekend		Date Read
Numbers	1/2 hour	_____
Numbers	1/2 hour	_____
Numbers	1/2 hour	_____

6th Weekend		Date Read
Numbers	1/2 hour	_____
Numbers	1/2 hour	_____
Numbers	1/2 hour	_____

7th Weekend		Date Read
Deuteronomy	1/2 hour	_____
Deuteronomy	1/2 hour	_____
Deuteronomy	1/2 hour	_____
Deuteronomy	1/2 hour	_____
Deuteronomy	1/2 hour	_____

8th Weekend		**Date Read**
Joshua	1/2 hour	_____
Joshua	1/2 hour	_____
Joshua	1/2 hour	_____
Joshua	1/2 hour	_____

9th Weekend		**Date Read**
Judges	1/2 hour	_____
Judges	1/2 hour	_____
Judges	1/2 hour	_____
Judges	1/2 hour	_____
Ruth	1/4 hour	_____

10th Weekend		**Date Read**
1 Samuel	1/2 hour	_____
1 Samuel	1/2 hour	_____
1 Samuel	1/2 hour	_____
1 Samuel	1/2 hour	_____
1 Samuel	1/2 hour	_____

11th Weekend		**Date Read**
2 Samuel	1/2 hour	_____
2 Samuel	1/2 hour	_____
2 Samuel	1/2 hour	_____
2 Samuel	1/2 hour	_____

12th Weekend		**Date Read**
1 Kings	1/2 hour	_____
1 Kings	1/2 hour	_____
1 Kings	1/2 hour	_____

13th Weekend		**Date Read**
2 Kings	1/2 hour	_____
2 Kings	1/2 hour	_____
2 Kings	1/2 hour	_____
2 Kings	1/2 hour	_____

14th Weekend		**Date Read**
1 Chronicles	1/2 hour	_____
1 Chronicles	1/2 hour	_____
1 Chronicles	1/2 hour	_____
1 Chronicles	1/2 hour	_____

15th Weekend		**Date Read**
2 Chronicles	1/2 hour	_____
2 Chronicles	1/2 hour	_____
2 Chronicles	1/2 hour	_____
2 Chronicles	1/2 hour	_____
2 Chronicles	1/2 hour	_____

16th Weekend		**Date Read**
Ezra	1/2 hour	_____
Ezra	1/2 hour	_____
Nehemiah	1/2 hour	_____
Nehemiah	1/2 hour	_____

17th Weekend		**Date Read**
Esther	1/2 hour	_____
Job	1/2 hour	_____
Job	1/2 hour	_____
Job	1/2 hour	_____
Job	1/2 hour	_____

18th Weekend		**Date Read**
Psalms	1/2 hour	_____
Psalms	1/2 hour	_____
Psalms	1/2 hour	_____
Psalms	1/2 hour	_____

19th Weekend		**Date Read**
Psalms	1/2 hour	_____
Psalms	1/2 hour	_____
Psalms	1/2 hour	_____
Psalms	1/2 hour	_____

20th Weekend		**Date Read**
Proverbs	1/2 hour	_____
Proverbs	1/2 hour	_____
Proverbs	1/2 hour	_____
Ecclesiastes	1/2 hour	_____
Song	1/4 hour	_____

21st Weekend		**Date Read**
Isaiah	1/2 hour	_____
Isaiah	1/2 hour	_____
Isaiah	1/2 hour	_____
Isaiah	1/2 hour	_____

22nd Weekend		**Date Read**
Isaiah	1/2 hour	_____
Isaiah	1/2 hour	_____
Isaiah	1/2 hour	_____

23rd Weekend		**Date Read**
Jeremiah	1/2 hour	_____
Jeremiah	1/2 hour	_____
Jeremiah	1/2 hour	_____
Jeremiah	1/2 hour	_____

24th Weekend		**Date Read**
Jeremiah	1/2 hour	_____
Jeremiah	1/2 hour	_____
Jeremiah	1/2 hour	_____
Jeremiah	1/2 hour	_____
Lamentations	1/4 hour	_____

25th Weekend		**Date Read**
Ezekiel	1/2 hour	_____
Ezekiel	1/2 hour	_____
Ezekiel	1/2 hour	_____
Ezekiel	1/2 hour	_____

26th Weekend		**Date Read**
Ezekiel	1/2 hour	_____
Ezekiel	1/2 hour	_____
Ezekiel	1/2 hour	_____

27th Weekend		**Date Read**
Daniel	1/2 hour	_____
Daniel	1/2 hour	_____
Daniel	1/2 hour	_____
Hosea	1/2 hour	_____

28th Weekend		**Date Read**
Joel	1/4 hour	_____
Amos	1/2 hour	_____
Obadiah	1/4 hour	_____
Jonah	1/4 hour	_____

29th Weekend		**Date Read**
Micah	1/4 hour	_____
Nahum	1/4 hour	_____
Habakkuk	1/4 hour	_____
Zephaniah	1/4 hour	_____

30th Weekend		**Date Read**
Haggai	1/4 hour	_____
Zechariah	1/2 hour	_____
Malachi	1/4 hour	_____

NEW TESTAMENT

31st Weekend		**Date Read**
Matthew	1/2 hour	_____
Matthew	1/2 hour	_____
Matthew	1/2 hour	_____
Matthew	1/2 hour	_____
Matthew	1/2 hour	_____

32nd Weekend		**Date Read**
Mark	1/2 hour	_____
Mark	1/2 hour	_____
Mark	1/2 hour	_____

33rd Weekend		**Date Read**
Luke	1/2 hour	_____
Luke	1/2 hour	_____
Luke	1/2 hour	_____
Luke	1/2 hour	_____
Luke	1/2 hour	_____

34th Weekend		**Date Read**
John	1/2 hour	_____
John	1/2 hour	_____
John	1/2 hour	_____
John	1/2 hour	_____

35th Weekend

		Date Read
Acts	1/2 hour	_____
Acts	1/2 hour	_____
Acts	1/2 hour	_____
Acts	1/2 hour	_____
Acts	1/2 hour	_____

36th Weekend

		Date Read
Romans	1/2 hour	_____
Romans	1/2 hour	_____
1 Corinthians	1/2 hour	_____
1 Corinthians	1/2 hour	_____

37th Weekend

		Date Read
2 Corinthians	1/2 hour	_____
2 Corinthians	1/2 hour	_____
Galatians	1/2 hour	_____
Ephesians	1/2 hour	_____

38th Weekend

		Date Read
Philippians	1/4 hour	_____
Colossians	1/4 hour	_____
1 Thessalonians	1/4 hour	_____
2 Thessalonians	1/4 hour	_____
1 Timothy	1/4 hour	_____
2 Timothy	1/4 hour	_____
Titus	1/4 hour	_____
Philemon	1/4 hour	_____

39th Weekend		**Date Read**
Hebrews	1/2 hour	_____
Hebrews	1/2 hour	_____
James	1/4 hour	_____
1 Peter	1/4 hour	_____
2 Peter	1/4 hour	_____
1 John	1/4 hour	_____
2 John	1/4 hour	_____
3 John	1/4 hour	_____
Jude	1/4 hour	_____

40th Weekend		**Date Read**
Revelation	1/2 hour	_____
Revelation	1/2 hour	_____
Revelation	1/2 hour	_____